D1391685

MODERN
AMERICAN
HISTORY ★ A
Garland
Series

Edited by
FRANK FREIDEL
Harvard University

ACADEMICIANS IN GOVERNMENT FROM ROOSEVELT TO ROOSEVELT

Paul B. Cook

Garland Publishing, Inc.
New York & London ★ 1982

Library of Congress Cataloging in Publication Data

Cook, Paul B., 1933–
    Academicians in government from Roosevelt to Roosevelt.

    (Modern American history ; MAH 24)
    Originally presented as the author's thesis (Ph.D.—
University of Kentucky)
    Bibliography: p.
    Includes index.
    1. Social scientists in government—United States—
History. I. Title.
H53.U5C66   1982   353'.0722   80-8470
ISBN 0-8240-4853-9   AACR2

All volumes in this series are printed on acid-free,
250-year-life paper.
Printed in the United States of America

TO

Rose, Sheryl, Paul Kelly, and Mrs. J. M. Cook

PREFACE

The extensive use of professors by President Franklin D. Roosevelt was viewed by many as a unique occurrence in American history. A study of the history of the nation beginning with the post-Civil War period reveals the presence of academicians in government service. The number increased in the early years of the twentieth century, and the New Deal was a highlight in this development.

A significant number of academicians was attracted to government service during the New Deal. This study treats this as the continuation of a trend rather than a one-time occurrence. The parameters and overview of the study are outlined in Chapter I.

The work was originally presented as part of the requirements for the doctorate at the University of Kentucky. I am grateful to the members of my advisory committee: Drs. Collins Burnett, Morris B. Cierley, Holman Hamilton, James F. Hopkins, and James B. Kincheloe. Dr. Burnett, Committee Chairman, provided encouragement, advice, and comfort during the preparation of the work. The late Dr. Hamilton was especially helpful as I attempted to develop a direction in my research and writing.

I am grateful to my wife, Rose, for her support of all my professional activities. To our children, Sheryl Lynn and Paul Kelly, I am grateful for their interest and support. My mother has been a constant source of support and encouragement, and for this I am thankful.

Paul B. Cook

TABLE OF CONTENTS

TABLE OF CONTENTS -- <u>Continued</u>

CHAPTER I

INTRODUCTION

President Franklin D. Roosevelt shocked many Americans in the early 1930's by placing academicians in prominent positions in the federal government. Academicians were still viewed by some people in America as being too visionary, impractical, and woolly-minded to occupy such important positions. The involvement of the academician in public service, culminating in the opportunity provided by the New Deal, is the subject of this study.

In addition to analyzing the factors that led to this involvement, the study identifies many of the prominent academicians who were drawn into government service from the time of the Presidency of Theodore Roosevelt until the pre-war years of Franklin D. Roosevelt's administration. Basic to the study is the idea that academicians as trustees of specialized information recognized their obligation to use or disseminate their acquired information for the improvement of society just as the possessors of material means employed their means for human betterment. The subject also lends itself to an interdisciplinary study which is in keeping with current trends in higher education.

Need for the Study

Even though the professor has been the subject of numerous studies, current investigation revealed no comprehensive study of the academician in government service as outlined in this work. Most of the literature related to the topic is centered around the involvement of academicians during World War I and in association with the depression. Claude C. Bowman made a similar observation regarding the involvement in government service by professors when he commented:

> It is only at certain periods that his participation becomes of sufficient popular interest to win the attention of the magazine editors but the less sensational activities of many professors in guiding the practical affairs of the nation constitute a long and, as yet, unwritten chapter (16, p. 145).

Much of the literature pertaining to the subject is filled with generalities about the role of the academician in public service. The following statement by Leonard D. White is typical of such a position. In a work published in 1933 he declared the following: "Conclusive evidence is not at hand to confirm the view that university men are participating more widely in public affairs than ten or twenty years ago; may the writer state on the basis of his own observation that such seems to be the case" (202, p. 327). In addition to surveying much of the material related to higher education and government service and to viewing social conditions this study will include more specific contributions which have emerged. Generalities such as White's are given some quantitative substance, and as a result the current void in the literature in higher education is partially filled. Existing attitudes and prevailing views concerning the role of the academician in American life in the 1920's are also questioned. The idea that academicians came to Washington only during crises is explored. Crises are treated as peaks in a continuous trend rather than as isolated high points.

Purpose of the Study

The purpose of this work is to examine the development of the utilitarian approach in higher education and the involvement of the academicians in public service beginning with the low ebb of service to government in the late 1800's. Within this context an effort is made to analyze conditions that led to the involvement of academicians at the national level. Among the factors analyzed is the need by government for expertise possessed by academicians brought about by the complexity of life resulting from industrial growth and economic expansion. The establishment of a trend toward government service is also explored by identifying many of those who rendered public service. The list is not exhaustive, but those who occupied important positions and those who performed significant advisery and consultant services are included.

Scope and Delimitations

No claim is made for all-inclusiveness, especially in regard to the identification of individuals involved. Sheer numbers prohibited the inclusion of all who could be considered proper candidates. The academic reputation of the individual and the significance of the service rendered were considered in the selection process. A large number of academicians are listed in the appendix in addition to those discussed in the body of the study.

The period under consideration began with the late nineteenth century and continued into the 1930's. These limitations were influenced
by events and were not arbitrarily selected. The points of origin are
purposefully vague since movements do not begin and end at exact times.
The study begins with the late nineteenth century since this was a time
during which the objectives of higher education were widely discussed
and the utilitarian and public service aspects began to be accepted.
The first years of the New Deal were selected as the termination point
because the pattern of public service was well established by that time
and because the trend toward public service was adequately demonstrated
in this time span.

The period since the thirties encompasses too much additional material for a study which includes the individuals involved. In addition,
the use of academicians by the government continued to increase after the
1930's. The service of academicians during the Second World War is widely recognized, and according to an editorial in Harper's Magazine (59,
p. 18) the Eisenhower administration employed more professors than the
New Deal. The status of academicians in government service by the 1960's
was recognized by Jacques Barzun, who commented: "By President Kennedy's
time the new order of things was a commonplace" (7, p. 51). President
Johnson continued the practice of drawing academicians into government
service. Finally, President Nixon's appointment of Clifford Hardin and
George Schultz to the cabinet, and the selection of Henry Kissinger and
Daniel P. Moynihan as presidential advisers further indicates that academicians will continue to have an opporunity to provide a vital service
to government.

Use of Terms

Many of the terms used in the study are clarified in the context in which they are used. However, some other terms require some clarification. Utilitarian is used in a sweeping social sense with the concept of public service at its vertex rather than in a strict vocational manner. Other terms could be substituted, but this term is used by other writers and seems to be appropriate here. The terms found most frequently in the literature relating to the individual are academician, intellectual, professor, service intellectual, and scholar. Professor is unsatisfactory, since individuals are included who earned doctorates but who never held a faculty appointment. The term intellectual did not come into use until the present century and is generally used to include a more diverse group than is treated in this work. Scholar, like the term intellectual, is often used in referring to a group that may include people other than professors. Academician, on the other hand, does not seem to be as restrictive as the other terms and tends to more clearly pinpoint the group under consideration.

The term expert is frequently used in reference to the academician. It is not the contention that academicians are the only experts but that many academicians who possessed expertise in given areas were called upon to render a service to government. Other academicians have not been looked upon as experts but have influenced public policy and public opinion as ideologists. In this regard Richard Hofstader pointed out that many intellectuals are not experts with an important role in public life and that many of them do not impinge very forcefully upon the public consciousness (94, p. 34). When the term <u>the government</u> is used, it refers to the federal government. References to other levels of government will be so indicated.

Overview of the Work

The work is divided into six chapters. The first includes the introduction to the study. Chapter II deals with background materials and sets the stage for developments in the twentieth century. It includes public service by academicians at state and local levels, and changes in society and corresponding changes in higher education prior to the twentieth century. Chapters III, IV, and V deal with the actual involvement of academicians and are generally centered around presidential administrations. This approach was selected primarily for organizational purposes; however, academicians are more associated with some adminstrations than others. There may be a more logical division of the material, but the grouping of the administrations within each of the chapters seems to be defensible. The material in Chapter III is centered around the Progressive Movement and includes the administrations of Presidents Theodore Roosevelt and William Howard Taft and the pre-war years of President Woodrow Wilson's administration. Chapter IV covers the years from the entry of the United States into World War I through President Herbert Hoover's administration. Chapter V includes the early years of Franklin D. Roosevelt's presidency. The concluding chapter is devoted to conclusions drawn from the study and recommendations for further study.

CHAPTER II

HIGHER EDUCATION AND THE DEVELOPMENT OF PUBLIC SERVICE

Mid-Eighteenth Century

In the post-Civil War period scholars were frequently indicted for their failure to contribute to the continuing growth of our civilization. Wendell Phillips in his Phi Beta Kappa address at Harvard in 1881 is frequently cited in this regard. Merle Curti quotes Phillips as stating the following:

> American scholars had dodged five great opportunities to align themselves with the forces of progress and humanity; in the slavery controversy, in penal reform, in the temperance crusade, in the women's movement, and in the labor struggle. Timid scholarship either shrinks from sharing in these agitations, or denounces them as vulgar and dangerous interference by incompetent hands with matters above them (45, p. 21).

Phillips was not the only one to condemn academicians for their attitude toward public service. James Russell Lowell, a service-oriented intellectual, belittled, ". . .picayunish scholarship that divorced itself from the larger culture and the larger life" (46, p. 18). Writing in the last decade of the past century, Lord Bryce observed that college professors were denounced by professional politicians as, ". . . unpractical, visionary, pharisaical, kid-gloved, high-toned, and un-American" (21, p. 304). From his vantage point in the twentieth century, Harold Stearns supported the position taken by Phillips, Lowell, and others. Stearns accused intellectuals in the last half of the nineteenth century

7

of devoting their energies to the sciences or academic speculation rather than attempting to bring their knowledge to bear upon practical social problems. He took the position that the social and political world at that time was so crude and raw that the intellectuals pursued the transcendental technique of escaping to an ivory tower. This is the period in which Stearns stated that the following attitude solidified: "Politics was considered something which a gentleman would, as he valued his reputation, diligently shun; the scholar turned from practical life with a kind of instinctive repugnance" (177, p.71). Stearns continued by observing that the scholars, artists, literary men, and philosophers tended to enjoy their abstract holiday rather than deal with the harsh forces at work in American life and that scholars tended to become "meticulous experts" (177, p. 76).

Before examining the validity and implications of these charges, a consideration of the attitudes and developments prior to the Civil War is beneficial. Richard Hofstadter noted that in the early years of our national existence the relationship between intellect and power was not a problem because the leaders were the intellectuals (94, p. 145). In this regard, Curti points out that many of the founders of the Republic combined scholarship and action. He supports the idea that the men at the Constitutional Convention of 1787 may be considered the first brain trust by noting that of the 55 members, two were university presidents, three were professors, and thirty-one had college educations (45, p. 15). From the Convention until the Civil War, persons generally considered intellectuals continued to play prominent roles in public affairs.

Thomas Jefferson, John Adams, John Quincy Adams, and James Madison were the more noted of this group in the decades following the writing of the Constitution.

The trend continued into the nineteenth century as shown by Washington Irving's service as minister to Spain; Nathaniel Hawthorne's service as American consul at Liverpool; and the public service efforts of William Austin, George Bancroft, Rufus Choate, Caleb Cushing, Alexander and Edward Everett, James Russell Lowell, George Perkins Marsh , and others (83, p. 105). Edward Everett's involvement in public service was extensive for any age, but especially for the nineteenth century. Following a successful career at Harvard, he served in the House of Representatives from 1825 to 1835 and was then elected governor of Massachusetts. Later he served as minister to England and Secretary of State. In 1860 he was a candidate for Vice President of the United States on the Constitutional Union ticket (64, pp. 623-27). Gurko stated that this involvement in public affairs emerged without any crystallized sentiment against these men. He pointed out that the attitude of the public toward academicians in this period may have resulted from "the illiteracy that prevailed among large sections of the population, with the consequent premium placed on the political services of those who had been formally educated" (83, p. 104).

By the nineteenth century the learned men in government did not constitute a large number, and of this group only a few could be considered academicians. However, the attitude of the public was more receptive toward academicians than in the later decades of the century.

According to one author, an equilibrium had been achieved between anti-intellectualism and respect for learning by the Civil War. William E. Leuchtenburg stated:

> There was very little hostility to a class of intellectuals; the men who worked in shops, or tilled the fields or ran for office did not think of men like Emerson or Whittier or Longfellow as representing a dangerous alien minority; they seemed as American as the next man. Men read the histories of Bancroft or crowded to the Chautauqua lectures of Massachusetts poets with a sense of sharing in a common American culture (119, p. 9).

However, as will be shown later, this spirit did not carry over into the post-Civil War era.

The rule of what has been referred to as the "patrician elite" (94, p. 146) in the late eighteenth and early nineteenth centuries soon gave way to a popular democracy. However, the rise of popular democracy should not receive all the blame for the decline in the regard for intellect in politics. The growth of party divisions, led in part by one as intellectual as Thomas Jefferson, was also a contributing factor. Hofstadter stated that the first significant movement against intellectuals in American politics was in conjunction with the Jacksonian era. According to Hofstadter this resulted from "Its distrust of expertise, its dislike for centralization, its desire to uproot the entrenched classes, and its doctrine that important functions were simple enough to be performed by anyone" (94, p. 155). This position repudiated government by gentlemen, the term used by Hofstadter which includes academicians (94, p. 156).

Some intellectuals were associated with President Jackson even though his administration was closely linked with the rise of popular democracy. George Bancroft was probably the most famous of the number, but Hofstadter contends that Jacksonian democracy failed to achieve the approachment between the intellectual and the popular mind that was later attained by progressivism and the New Deal (94, p. 157).

At no time in our history is there a clear demarcation between peak periods of involvement of academicians in performing public service and periods of limited participation or exclusion. The Civil War is more nearly a dividing point than any other, and as a result the years before and after are transitional periods and difficult to describe. The role of the academician in public service at the mid-point of the nineteenth century was undergoing a transition. In the 1840's and 1850's geological surveys were conducted; roads, canals, and railroads were constructed; and municipalities were beginning to show concern for water supply, sewage disposal, and other problems (45, p. 19). All of these required experts and not the type of person who had served as adviser or minister to a foreign country. But as Hofstadter stated, even the expert was restricted by the Civil War. He said:

> Just as the gentleman was being elbowed out of the way by the homely necessities of American elections, the expert, even the merely competent man, was being restricted by the demands of the party system and the creed of rotation into a sharply limited place in the American political system (94, p. 171).

The academician had been relegated to a marginal role and generally alienated from politics in the United States by mid-century.

Post-Civil War Era

Unlike the wars in the twentieth century, the Civil War did not
enhance the status of academicians. The World Wars placed a premium on
industrial and technical know-how which required learned men. By contrast, the changes in society produced partially by the Civil War caused
the ivory tower to be more attractive to the academician. The usual
arguments against men of theory participating in government were given
in this period. These included the idea that there was a dichotomy between theory and action and that those who knew the theory were too
visionary and impractical to be given responsible positions in government. Gurko supports this position in the observation that since
Benjamin Franklin's day our experiences, "including the frontier, the
immense growth of industrial technology, and the global wars of the
twentieth century, have confirmed and solidified our attachment to the
practical" (83, p. xiv).

This view was strengthened by the materialistic outlook that en-
gulfed the business interests of the nation. The following statement
concerning the businessmen illustrates this idea: "The new generation
of entrepreneurs was more voracious than the old, and politics appeared
to have been abandoned to bloody-shirt demogogy, to dispensing the
public domain to railroad barons, and to the tariff swindle" (94, p. 172).
Men of ideas, who thought first and then acted, were probably more out
of place in this period than in any other. This attitude was brought to
a head by the enormous wealth of the country which was gained by those
who moved most swiftly. Gurko states that the growth of industry

following the war helped to break up the degree of fusion of theory and practice that previously existed and created a great imbalance in favor of practicality and material values (83, P. 106).

Henry Adams, one of America's leading intellectuals in the post-Civil War era, recognized the trend that was underway in the nation. In 1870, Adams moved from Washington to accept a teaching position at Harvard. In a letter to C. M. Gaskell he gave an indication for wanting to leave Washington: "All my friends have been or are on the point of being driven out of the government and I should have been left without any allies or sources of information" (94, p. 173). Lord Bryce's visits to the United States produced a similar reaction. He observed that birth and education gave a man little advantage in politics and caused the finest or most ambitious spirits to pursue other careers and leave politics to men of second order (21, p. 228).

With this background in mind, it is possible to more thoroughly evaluate the indictments of American academicians by Phillips, Lowell, and others. Their charge that academicians were not concerned with the remainder of society is accurate to a certain extent. Academicians were not extensively engaging in public service during this period, but neither did they totally withdraw from serving the public. It is not the objective of this study to explore in depth the activities of academicians during this era but to observe it as background for the twentieth century so that the timing of the remarks by Phillips and Lowell holds significance for this study. About the time these statements were being made forces were at work that would come to fruition in the twentieth century. As a result the range of activities open to academicians was significantly expanded. Some forces affected society, and these produced changes in higher education. Academicians were, in turn, influenced by societal and educational changes.

This study will not attempt to deal with all the changes that characterized higher education in the late nineteenth century. The changes were too extensive to be treated thoroughly in such a study. Laurence Veysey indicates the scope of these changes in the following statement: "The American university of 1900 was all but unrecognizable in comparison with the college of 1860" (194, p. 2). Secondly, due to the nature of this study, the primary concern is with the development of a utilitarian approach in the curriculum and public service, or, as Curti refers to these developments, the "secularization of scholarship" (46).

The transformation in higher education following the war was deeply influenced by the first Morrill Act and the many other events during the war. Brubacher and Rudy view the war as a catalyst in this regard. Concerning the catalytic role of the war they stated: "It was such a thorough--going social convulsion that it forced American academicians to recognize, once and for all, the professional respectability and social indispensability of the engineer, the natural scientist, and the industrial technician" (20, p. 109). They suggest that with this recognition, training for the careers had to be provided and placed in the curriculum parallel with old programs for educating ministers, physicians, and lawyers. Industrial expansion that followed the war reinforced this trend (20, p. 109). The development and growth of the elective principle in the college curriculum was very important to the emergence of the public service idea.

Public Service

As previously suggested, the growth of the state universities was a distinguishing feature of higher education in the post-Civil War period. The state universities, primarily in the Mid-west and West, provided the impetus for the development of utilitarianism and public service. Near the end of the past century the attitude of the general public toward higher education was skeptical and frequently contemptuous. Since that time there has been an important shift in public opinion. State universities deserve much of the credit for this change because of their democratization of higher education and their efforts toward public service. Because the element of public service is central in this investigation, considerable space is devoted to developments in state universities and to the factors that led to a sound basis for the academician providing service to the government by 1900.

The American state university came into existence in the South in the late eighteenth century, but not in the form that we are familiar with today. In the first half of the nineteenth century additional state universities were established in the West. It was in this section of the country that state institutions flourished after the war. Even though the University of Wisconsin ultimately got the major portion of the credit for public service, the University of Michigan was the pacemaker in the West in much the same manner that the University of Virginia had been in the ante-bellum South. Michigan's charter was used as the pattern for establishing the University of Minnesota in 1851, and it appears to have influenced the decisions of the men who drafted the charter for the University of Wisconsin (20, p. 156). Frederick Rudolph agrees with many of the writers that the state universities were shaped in the Mid-west and West. Rudolph noted the significance of the setting by pointing out that this was where "frontier democracy and frontier materialism would help to support a practical--oriented popular institution" (166, p. 377).

Universities in the West had the examples of the Universities of Virginia and Michigan to emulate in developing curricula. Emigrants from the New England states provided leadership in some instances. This was especially true at the University of Minnesota. Foreign attitudes toward higher education were also influential in the institutions of higher learning in the interior of America. The French idea of centralization was of limited importance as compared with the Germanic idea of service that characterized these budding institutions. But the most important stimulus to the establishment of state universities was the granting of public land by the federal government. In the Old Northwest this can be traced from Manasseh Cutler in the post-Revolutionary War era to the Land Ordinance of 1787, to the Land Grant Acts of 1862 and 1890 (20, pp. 153-54).

Frederick Jackson Turner, the noted frontier historian, also suggested some reasons for the direction taken by western universities. The universities had a duty to adjust pioneer ideals to the new requirements of American democracy, and in this they contributed to the assimilation of peoples and ideas (188, p. 287). Turner also emphasized the practical nature of the area: "The West laid emphasis upon the practical and demanded that ideals should be put to work for useful ends; ideals were tested by their direct contributions to the betterment of the average man, rather than by the production of the man of exceptional genius and distinction" (188, p. 355). In a commencement address at Indiana University in 1910, Turner stated that one of the most striking features of our educational history was the constant pressure of democracy upon the universities to adapt to the requirements of all the people. The universities of the Middle West, molded under pioneer ideals, produced a fuller recognition of scientific studies, especially the applied sciences, as related to the conquest of nature; the movement away from the required curriculum; the offering of vocational and college work in the same institution; the development of colleges of agriculture and engineering; and the training of lawyers, journalists, public men, and administrators. Institutions in other parts of the country were performing many or all of these functions, but, as Turner observed, universities in the Middle West stressed the ideal of service to democracy rather than of individual advancement alone (188, p. 283).

It has been suggested that the identification of state universities with a state or region emerged as each particular area developed. This became more apparent as higher education spread westward and as the country grew larger. Expansion in higher education coincided with the trend toward a more practical minded outlook by the nation, which resulted in academic works becoming increasingly utilitarian. However, it should be noted that while these developments were taking place in state universities in the West, public and private institutions in the East were also moving toward a utilitarian approach. It is also interesting to observe that when academicians became a widely accepted part of government, a large number came from private colleges and universities, some of which were located in the East. R. Freeman Butts suggested such an idea in his noted work on higher education when he stated:

> Again, with caution as to the validity of such generaliza-
> tions, it might be said that with the exception of the
> large institutions of the East, the democratic movement in
> higher education gained its most rapid headway in connection
> with the state universities of the Middle West and Far West
> (27, p. 225).

This point will be illustrated in the chapters that follow.

Development of Utilitarianism

The movement toward utilitarianism has several aspects and could be approached from more than one angle. The approach used here is to trace historically the forces that contributed to curricular changes and to show their culmination near the end of the century. Charles K. Adams, president of the University of Wisconsin, declared in 1897 that indictments such as those of Wendell Phillips could not have been fairly leveled at the state universities (46, p. 18). Adams was justified in making this response because state universities in particular had been moving toward a public service posture for decades. A brief review of the developments at the University of Virginia and at Harvard reveals such a posture. The origin of public service in the United States may be traced to Jefferson and the University of Virginia. John S. Brubacher and Willis Rudy, in their thorough history of American higher education, link utility and the development of the elective system together and consider these and other aspects as curricular reforms. They consider the controversies surrounding the elective system as the central educational battle of the nineteenth century (20). Since the combining of these two aspects of higher education seems to be a plausible approach, they will be considered jointly.

When the University of Virginia opened in 1825, students were to be free to choose the lectures they wished to attend. A close observer of the Virginia plan was George Ticknor of Harvard. Ticknor was unable to bring about such a radical departure at Harvard, and Virginia soon modified its plan; however, efforts to liberalize the curriculum produced a chain reaction in colleges that climaxed many years later (10, p. 101). The experiments with electives were dealt a near fatal blow by the Yale Report of 1828, which staunchly supported the classical curriculum. Brubacher and Rudy commented: "As a thoroughgoing defense of the traditional American liberal-arts college, it gave heart to academic conservatives everywhere" (20, p. 103). In the years following the Yale Report, curriculum reformers did not rest. Francis Wayland, president of Brown University, soundly indicted conservatism and struck out at those who opposed changes in the curriculum and embraced the traditional approaches. Prior to becoming president of the University of Michigan, Henry Philip

Tappan unsuccessfully worked for curriculum reform. When he became president at Michigan he saw great possibilities. He is credited with having "visions of a sort of New World version of the University of Berlin, devoted to the advancement of learning and specialized research, which would flower under his guidance in the Valley of Democracy" (20, p. 106). Tappan realized a need for changes and revealed his German training in making one of the earliest calls for public service.

The most significant development in connection with the elective curriculum occurred at Harvard in the late 1860's. The adoption of the elective principle was under Charles W. Eliot's leadership, but it probably would not have been accomplished so soon without the earlier work of Ticknor and others. The elective curriculum was adopted by other institutions in varying forms, and by 1900 was enjoying wide-spread support. Resources and ideologies were the major factors influencing the extent of the elective principle, but Frederick Rudolph noted its importance at state universities by 1900: "Unquestionably the large state universities of the Midwest and West, with their commitment to public service and to learning, were more friendly than any other group of institutions to the elective principle" (166, p. 303).

State universities were an integral part of the university building movement which flourished after the Civil War. The role they played is indicated by the fact that four of the eight universities with enrollments of 2,500 or over by 1900 were state institutions (20, p. 159). A number of factors contributed to this growth. The federal government gave public higher education an important stimulus with financial grants through the Morrill Acts of 1862 and 1890. The actual amount of money received varied in large measure according to the way in which the grant was administered (166, p. 252). Strong public demand for broad, inclusive, all-purpose training also contributed to the growth of state institutions. Such a request resulted from the social and economic changes associated with the growing specialization in most aspects of life. The universities were in an admirable position to offer the services requested (20, p. 159).

Another factor responsible for this growth was the industrial revolution. The importance of this factor is apparent when one considers the demand that the new sciences be applied to the development of the nation's resources. The state universities appeared to be the ideal vehicle for accelerating this process. The growth of state universities was also encouraged by the rapid expansion of the public school system (20, pp. 160-61).

Allan Nevins viewed the changes associated with higher education after the Civil War as a revolt centered around the "rejection of the tyranny of classical and theological studies, championship of science, insistence on attention to agriculture and the mechanical arts, and--most important of all--a demand for greater democracy in education" (146, p. 2). The demand for changes was voiced by individuals in many walks of life. Prior to becoming President of the United States, James A. Garfield advocated curricular revisions. He accused colleges and universities of placing in one end of the balance all of the mathematical studies, all the physical sciences, the principles of political economy and social science, the history of our nation, the constitution of government, and the literature and the history of modern civilizations and kicking the beam when Greece and Rome were placed in the other balance (145, p. 6).

Nevins stated that by 1887 or thereabouts leading public universities began to strive for new objectives. They began to make themselves useful to their states, not in the traditional avenues, but in new ways, becoming, in the words of an English university leader "community service centers " (145, p. 78). They began a concentration on teaching open thought and analysis, and placed less emphasis on facts. The preparation of people for specialized fields was beginning to be stressed.

State universities may have been in the forefront of these changes because they were tax supported. Public institutions came to be regarded as public property, as bodies whose objective was service to the state rather than service to the individual. This attitude carries through the democratized concept of education that was supported by Jefferson (148, p. 157). Charles R. Van Hise expressed a similar view in 1916: "The state owns the university; and every citizen feels himself to be a stockholder in that ownership" (190, p. 70).

Social Sciences

Another element that was essential before the universities could provide the services required of them in the twentieth century was the training of social scientists. Academic social science in the United States may be dated from the inauguration of Critical Investigations in History and Politics in 1876 at the newly formed The Johns Hopkins

University. About four years later, the School of Political Science was organized at Columbia University. These beginnings were followed by graduate instruction in history and related subjects at Harvard, Michigan, Pennsylvania, and Wisconsin (46, p. 41).

Andrew D. White, president of Cornell University, wrote Charles K. Adams in 1878 and indicated his interest in offering work in the social studies. He said: "I mean to devote myself to establishing at Cornell and urging the establishment everywhere of departments for the instruction especially of those who intend entering public life" (161, p. 131). He indicated that such departments might be called the departments of History, Political Science, and General Jurisprudence, and proposed a four-year undergraduate program (161, p. 131). There was opposition to placing some of the social sciences on an equal footing with established offerings. But from the standpoint of institutions of higher learning accepting the social sciences, perhaps no event is more significant than the founding of the University of Chicago in 1892. From the very beginning there was incorporated into the institution a full complement of departments offering graduate instruction and research in all of the social science disciplines (46, p. 42).

Many of the professors in the social sciences received their graduate training at German universities and observed German professors serving the state. For most this application of theory to practical problems was a new experience. Richard T. Ely stated: "My experience in Germany had first brought to my attention the importance of linking book knowledge and practical experience" (62, p. 187). Around 1900

there was an idea among German students that influenced Americans studying in German universities. The idea was that of the total number that
entered the university, one-third broke down, one-third went to the devil,
and the remaining one-third governed Europe (153, p. 658). American students did not return with the desire to rule, but they acquired a deep
interest in public service which, according to an American professor, was
the essence of German education: "The German idea of education begins
with the idea of service to humanity"(185, p. 59). When a German came
into the world it was not to live or make a brilliant career for himself
alone; he was also to be concerned about advancing human well-being as a
whole (185, p. 59).

The fusion of German ideas and American traditions was not an easy
matter and may have been the source of much of the disagreement among
professors in the social sciences in the late nineteenth century. In
spite of this disagreement, professors who subscribed to the German
ideas of research and public service made a tremendous impact on American higher education. Included in this number were Richard T. Ely,
Herbert B. Adams, John W. Burgess, Albion Small, and many others who in-
culcated students in the emerging graduate programs throughout the
United States with the concept of service to the state. Jurgen Herbst,
in his recent study, The German Historical School in American Scholarship,
drew some interesting conclusions concerning the German influence: "Like
their German colleagues, the American professors not only believed in
action, but exulted in it, and as in Germany, they were at home in the
new universities that had been founded at the centers of economic, social,

and political life" (89, p. 162). It was under these kinds of conditions
that leadership and participation in economics, politics, and social reform became a reality for the American academician. The trend became
more significant in the twentieth century, but the American social
scientists tended to sever their connections with the German professors.
Foreign affairs were partly responsible for the shift, but Americans also
moved away from collectivistic theories supported by the Germans. Herbst
suggested that the most important difference as far as public service was
concerned was that the American social scientist tended to be a pragmatist as opposed to the German historicist. The American could supply a
logical connection between scholarship and reform, between thought and
action, which the German had failed to do (89, p. 158).

On most university faculties the most vigorous supporters of public
service were the professors in the new applied sciences and a majority of
the social scientists. The academicians in the applied sciences did not
encounter the problems faced by the social scientists in attempting to
perform public service. Walter Lippmann, noted this paradox by suggesting that the man holding a public office knew that he needed help but
was reluctant to call in the social scientist, while the chemist, the
physicist, and the geologist had an earlier and more friendly reception
in government circles. The answer may be in the inability of the social
scientist to prove his work in the laboratory (127, p. 371). Hofstadter
also recognized the secondary position of the social scientist. He
summarized the position in the following statement: "The advice of experts in the physical sciences, however suspect many of these may be,

is accepted as indispensable. Expertise in the social sciences, on the
other hand, may be rejected as gratuitous and foolish, if not ominous"
(94, p. 36).

The rise of the social sciences nevertheless had a significant impact on American society. This idea is reflected in the following statement by William E. Leuchtenburg:

> Not only did the social scientist challenge many of the most
> hallowed ideas of American society such as the sanctity of
> the Constitution and the wisdom of a laissez-faire economy,
> but he brought into being a new career group which challenged
> the supremacy of the business man and the politician: the
> government administrator (119, p. 12).

These administrators will be studied in detail in the chapters that follow.

There was a gap of a generation before the full political impact of
the social scientists and the products of a utilitarian curriculum were
felt. In fact, the full force of the new social groups was not felt on
the national level until the creation of the brain trust by Franklin D.
Roosevelt in the 1932 campaign and during the first years of his administration. This supports the position stated previously that academicians
began to take steps in the late nineteenth century which paved the way
for the opportunities opened up to them by Franklin D. Roosevelt in the
1930's.

The new wave of learned societies that emerged in the late nineteenth century also contributed to the growth of the idea of public
service. Such societies as the American Economics Association, American
Historical Society, and others promoted professionalism and strengthened
the newer studies--especially the social sciences. The annual meetings

of the associations and their journals provided avenues for communication. In general, this development of professionalism paralleled the rise of the utility-oriented university and contributed to the concept of public service.

The rhetoric in support of academic public service quickened in the last two decades of the nineteenth century. As previously mentioned, Tappan called for public service as early as the 1850's, and Charles W. Eliot indicated an affinity for practical education when discussing the question "What can I do with my boy?" His answer was, "I wanted to give him a practical education; one that will prepare him, better than I was prepared, to follow my business, or any other active calling" (60, p. 203). President William W. Folwell of Minnesota favored a plan similar to White's at Cornell. Among other things it would be concerned with service to the needs of society through the study of government, commerce, and human relations. He envisioned a university which would train experts in public administration and legislation (20, p. 164).

At the 1898 meeting of the National Education Association, President Andrew S. Draper of the University of Illinois discussed the concern that colleges and universities should have for public questions. He took the position that the broader area of ethical thought and new economic and social conditions would cause states to set up universities and that these universities would be distinguished at an early date for their work dealing with public questions. Draper declared that in some instances state universities were attacking these issues in a manner that was most encouraging. Using a vernacular that could not have been encouraging to a practical-minded man, he summarized the possible effects of public service in these words: "The political science of a cosmopolitan and self-governing people may well have the leavening and leveling influence of independent and democratic universities" (54, pp. 114-15).

Writing in the Educational Review in 1898, William T. Harris emphasized the growing importance of advanced college work for dealing with problems in society. Harris had served as a teacher and administrator, and by 1900 was U. S. Commissioner of Education. He stated that a student who earned a doctor's degree could apply his knowledge to the problems of the nation. Harris then listed the problems that trained people are needed to handle: population growth, diplomacy, social and political problems at home, inventions, and a reconciliation of conflicting ideas in our environment. To Harris higher education was the only recourse for providing solutions to these pressing problems in our national life (87, pp. 160-61).

A strong plea for public service by state universities was made by Richard Henry Jesse, president of the University of Missouri. Jesse presented these views in an address before the National Education Association's annual meeting in 1901, which was two years before Van Hise became president of the University of Wisconsin. This indicated that universities in addition to Wisconsin were thinking along the lines of public service. Jesse suggested that the idea of the state caring for the university had been strenuously preached but that the reverse view was scarcely broached. This could be accomplished in material, social, political, and spiritual matters; for example, a college of agriculture could look after the material welfare of the people. He challenged the universities to collaborate with state boards, commissions, and bureaus

in improving social and economic conditions. Jesse encouraged sociologists to visit penal institutions and study existing conditions and
suggested that they also take up the problem of municipal taxation (108).

In a statement that sounded like a mid-twentieth century utterance,
he accused the universities of adhering too closely to the paths pre-
scribed by the federal government in the Hatch Act. Jesse charged that
except under federal leadership little had been done in the realm of
service to society. Academicians were given a very forceful challenge
by Jesse to utilize their knowledge for the betterment of society. He
concluded by outlining the overall functions of a university; these
functions were to investigate, to teach, and to publish (108, pp. 608-
09). In the discussion that followed the address, President William
L. Prather of the University of Texas called attention to services academicians were providing in his state, even though the legislators
thought the professors were theorists. The view of the university as
the guardian of the state was western in origin and to Prather could not
have developed in the East. He declared that it took time to create conditions favorable to public service, but that the day of prejudices
against the educational forces was passing. (108, p. 612).

In 1900, H. S. Pritchett became president of Massachusetts Institute
of Technology, after serving as Superintendent of the United States Coast
and Geodetic Survey. Because of his background Pritchett's statements
should have been very meaningful to the service-minded academician. By
this date he had observed that the government was turning more and more
to educated men for expert service. This service was not confined to

scientific experts but included men whose training placed them in a position to provide advice and assistance in many problem areas. He cited the work of academicians on the Philippine Commission as proof of opportunities for service provided by government (152, p. 658). Pritchett also called for a change of attitude by the academicians. Not only should the academician be better trained than his neighbor but more patriotic, more courageous, more informed concerning the service of the state, and more ready to take up its service. His contention was that "until such a spirit is a part of our system of higher education, that system will not have served the ends which education should service in a free state and for a free people" (152, p. 664).

In 1905, Edmund J. James was inaugurated president of the University of Illinois. He set forth his views on the role of public higher education in his inaugural address. James visualized state universities as becoming "more and more a great civil service of the state, the county, the municipality and the township, exactly as the military and naval academies are preparing young men for the military service of the government" (106, p. 625). The new president also observed that state universities were destined to become to an increasing degree the scientific arm of state government (106, p. 627). James' address supports the assumption that as the business of government became more complex and more difficult, the state university was the natural place to work on these problems (106).

The rhetoric for public service was not confined to university presidents. Frederick J. Turner called for training in science, law, politics, economics, and history to provide legislators, judges, and experts for commissions who could disinterestedly and intelligently mediate between contending interests (188, p. 285). By the last decade of the nineteenth century, magazines also began to support the concept of public service through editorials and articles.

As the foregoing statements have indicated, the interest in public service went beyond words and academicians were beginning to match deeds with words. Curti stated that this had become apparent by the 1880's, and that "Political scientists, economists, and sociologists joined hands with humanitarians in applying new knowledge about physical and mental health, housing, recreation, industrial accidents, and the exploitation of natural resources" (45, p. 26). It is not implied that all of these people by any means came from college and university faculties, but certainly some of them did and the number increased as the years passed. Some of the academicians, especially younger social scientists, moved faster than university presidents had intended. They saw corruption originating in private enterprise, at least in its monopolistic form, and to them this necessitated a change. As a result a peculiar relationship developed between the advocates of social utility and the advocates of social change (194, p. 73). This proved to be a point of irritation for many college and university presidents and a considerable concern in some cases, since the benefactors of the university were the object of the reformers. In this regard, Veysey stated, "The service-oriented university president and the faculty radical both agreed that what they called real life was the prime concern to academic men." Agreement on this point explained their basic partnership. Society could be served by offering training for success in the existing conditions or work to change the conditions (194, p. 73).

Assessment at the End of the Century

It would be erroneous to give the impression that utilitarianism and public service had the total support of the academic community by 1900. The utilitarian outlook advanced rapidly following the Civil War and claimed the support of many prominent academicians, but equally prominent men in higher education were not converted to the worth of public service and utilitarianism. In an article published in the Mississippi Valley Historical Review, Veysey made a strong case for four well-marked positions with regard to the programs and purposes of higher education as of 1900. Admittedly, all academicians could not be classified in four categories, but these seemed to be the major positions taken by academic leaders. One of the groups suggested by the author was composed of educational leaders who identified themselves with colleges as they existed in the mid-nineteenth century. They were true academic conservatives subscribing to the concept of mental discipline and religious piety. James McCash and Francis L. Patton were the most noted of this group. A second position began to gain momentum in the late 1860's. Veysey uses the term utility to describe this position. Its defenders advocated usefulness to the non-academic society, practical training, and a curriculum with all subjects placed on an equal basis. They favored the elective principle, and liked to talk about democracy as a desirable characteristic of higher education. Training for citizenship and for a skilled vocation were considered legitimate functions of the undergraduate program. Charles W. Eliot and Andrew D. White were the central figures in this movement. Unlike the following group they did not look to the German universities for inspiration, but built upon features and conditions that were indigenous to the United States (193, pp. 615-16).

During the 1870's and 1880's a group of reformers appeared in academic circles advocating scientific research as the primary educational purpose. Many of these academicians had earned Ph. D. degrees in Germany, and their emergence coincided with the development of graduate schools in the United States. The first institutions associated with this ideal were The Johns Hopkins University and Clark University and later Harvard, Columbia, and Chicago. The fourth outlook is most often referred to as "liberal culture." Advocates of this position opposed the elective system and specialization either in the form of vocational training or abstract research. Rather, they favored offering all students a broad training in literature, philosophy, and political science. Leaders in the liberal culture movement included Woodrow Wilson and A. Lawrence Lowell. Like the advocates of practical utility, they were concerned with the relation between the university and the social and political scene, but their methods of attack were quite different. Advocates of liberal culture wanted to educate future leaders in a common pattern and produce gentlemen to be concerned with the commonwealth (193, pp. 616-17).

Of these four positions, utility and research were predominant by 1900. Professors with loyalty to research did not take a very important part in public service at the turn of the century. Utilitarianism tended to develop in two wings in the late 1800's. Eliot was the leader of the wing in the East, and the wing in the West was inspired by President White of Cornell and, to a lesser degree, by leaders at the University of Michigan. Quantitatively the one in the West proved to be more important (194, p. 98). It is apparent that at the turn of the century there were many leaders in higher education who did not support the utilitarian concept. Nevertheless, the advocates of utilitarianism were in a position to make significant headway in the twentieth century.

The first decade of the twentieth century witnessed a reassessment of programs and purposes in higher education. By the end of the decade a new leadership had emerged, since most of the leaders in the post-Civil War period were in the grave or in retirement. Advocates of utilitarianism and research had gained ground in the colleges and universities, and as one writer suggested they had found a meeting ground of sorts:

> By 1910 utility and research uneasily joined together, held sway at most major institutions away from the eastern seaboard, but in so bland and official a fashion as to discourage the more ardent professional advocates of social change, on the one hand, and of pure investigation on the other (194, p. 257).

Twentieth Century Developments

By the twentieth century a significant segment of the academic
community was converted to utilitarianism and the larger society was
beginning to acknowledge the need for the service of academicians.
This, in turn, created a concern for the role that the individual
academicians would play in public service. It appears that an academician with political aspirations for public service is limited to
two basic choices in our system. He may pursue the elective route or
influence policy through expert analysis and advice. The first choice
has not been exercised very extensively, especially in national politics. In the period under consideration, some of the academicians
elected to the Congress were Henry Cabot Lodge, Samuel Fess, and Hiram
Bingham. In addition, Woodrow Wilson, Theodore Roosevelt, and William
Howard Taft could be given some consideration as academicians prior to
their becoming president. A few were also elected to governorships;
but the most success with the voters was at the state and local levels,
and even at these levels academicians found it difficult to successfully
compete with the politicians. Undoubtedly the situation that existed in
Connecticut in the fall of 1932 was an exception. Five professors were
candidates for office in the state, in addition to Yale's former foot-
ball coach seeking the office of Congressman. These men may have been
motivated by the success of other academicians in their state. Hiram
Bingham of Yale's Department of History was elected governor and United
States senator in 1924. He chose the seat in the Senate and then was
elected for a full term in 1926. In 1930 the dean of the Yale Graduate

school, Wilbur L. Cross, was elected governor. The tangle in 1932 is
illustrated by the following statement from School and Society:

> Opposing him (Hiram Bingham), in a rebellious wing of
> the Republican Party, is Professor Milton C. Conover,
> of the Political Science Department of Yale. Support-
> ing Professor Conover, and himself candidate for
> Governor, is Professor Albert Levitt, late of the
> Brooklyn College of Law, who, at the Independent
> Republican Convention, was nominated by Professor
> Irving Fisher, of the Economics Department of Yale.
> Professor Charles M. Bakewell, of the Yale Philosophy
> Department, is the regular Republican candidate for
> Congressman-at-large (153, p. 430).

Overall the number casting their lot with the voters has been small as
compared with those who pursued a non-elective route.

William E. Dodd, historian at the University of Chicago, recognized
the unique position of the academician in politics. A recent biographer
of Dodd, Robert Dallek, makes the following observation in this connection:

> Although Dodd in fact considered the elevation of academics
> like himself to public office a good idea, he was not being
> disingenuous. In his day it was a well-established, if
> somewhat declining, tradition of American academic life
> that professors cloak or conceal their ambitions, parti-
> cularly if they ranged beyond the confines of university
> or college work (50, p. 47).

Even though Dodd recognized the secondary position of academicians in
politics, he frequently became involved in direct political action.
After an unsuccessful effort to influence the decision of the Democratic
Party in the preconvention days of 1920, he acknowledged that "there
is little chance that an academic can influence party leadership" (50,
p. 122). Those academicians who attained national office will be considered in the following chapters.

Most service-oriented academicians chose to serve as advisers and to serve in the role of expert. A brief analysis of this role helps to explain the acceptance of the academicians by government and to explain partly the reaction of Americans to President Franklin D. Roosevelt's advisers. The expert came into use in the late nineteenth and early twentieth centuries at the local and state levels. As greater use was made of boards, commissions, and agencies it was necessary to have members and supportive staff who did not have a vested interest and who were at the same time competently trained to gather and analyze data. Academicians were not the only members of society who could perform such functions, but they constituted one of the available groups.

Writing in 1912 concerning the need for academicians in state government in Wisconsin, Charles McCarthy said that the times called for educated leaders: "General experience and rule-of-thumb information are inadequate for the solution of the problems of a democracy which no longer owns the safety fund of an unlimited quantity of untouched resources" (131, p. 125). Reinhold Niebuhr in discussing Walter Lippman and his age set forth the idea of academicians serving as a companion force to the elected officials. In his opinion the elected officials constituted a natural political aristocracy, but in a democracy other elite groups should be created. One of these would be composed of knowledgeable men who could aid the elected aristocracy (30,p. 174). In the same work, Arthur M. Schlesinger, Jr. declared that the experts "must confine themselves to the production of data for policymaking; they must themselves stay rigorously out of policy." He then quoted

Lippmann on the same point as saying, "The power of the expert depends upon separating himself from those who make the decisions, upon not caring, in his expert self, what decision is made." The role was changing from a philosophical one to serving up neutral facts to the ruling elite (30,p. 203).

A. N. Christensen and E. M. Kirkpatrick point out that the university expert can make a vital contribution when he is able to find his way around in public affairs. The background of the academician qualifies him to provide the politician with assistance on monetary, economic, and other technical questions. The respective roles as viewed by Christensen and Kirkpatrick are explained in the following statements: "It boils down to the point that good experts can make good ammunition but it is the politician who shoots it and knows when. The politician takes dough from the expert, but if it ever becomes well-baked bread, it will be in the politician's oven" (31, p. 18). However both men recognized the importance of the experts in government as public affairs became increasingly dominated by economic and technical forces.

Many of the academicians acknowledged that the university expert should not be placed in a command position. In a letter to Claude Kitchen in 1916, Professor Dodd noted that statisticians and economists would be indispensable for most areas but that he was opposed to turning things over to them entirely. His view was that specialists might prefer to serve their specialty rather than the public (50, p. 87). Professor William Yandell Elliott reluctantly agreed that academicians were probably better suited for advisery than for administrative work.

However, in defense of administrative roles for academicians, he stated that the record of college presidents would indicate that good administrators are produced through the college ranks about as often as by any other source. But in the final analysis, he agreed that academicians were more needed to think out conditions of solution than to execute them (61, p. 224).

John R. Commons, an economist and one of the earliest academicians to make his expertise available to the government, recognized that he was to serve only in an advisory capacity. In this regard he said that he learned that "the place of the economist was that of advisor to the leaders, if they wanted him, and not that of propagandist to the masses" (38, p. 110). Political leaders had experienced success and defeat, so they knew how much material they could use. Therefore, Commons provided the leaders with the information which they used to the best of their judgement, and he accepted philosophically the rejection of parts of his work. Concerning his service to the state of Wisconsin he stated: "I never initiated anything. I came only on request of legislators, of executives, or committees of the legislature." In Commons' opinion this attitude characterized most of the faculty at the University of Wisconsin. As a result of the highly independent nature of professors and the differences of opinion on any faculty, Commons noted that a professor

> can furnish only technical details and then only when he is wanted by politicians who really govern the state. So with the brain trust at Washington. I see individuals coming and going according to whether or not they furnish the President with what he wants. A different president has a different brain trust (38, p. 110).

These comments, incorporated in his autobiography published in 1934, seem to reflect the analysis of a man who was actively involved in public service at all levels of government for about three decades.

Another serviced-minded academician, Felix Frankfurter, believed the disinterested expert was important to our system. Schlesinger stated that Frankfurter was "deeply impressed by the intricate problems thrown up by industrial civilization; merely to analyze these issues requires a vast body of technical knowledge" (170, p. 223). Frankfurter, along with others, viewed the need for academicians in government resulting partly from the lack of a civil service system such as the British developed. He declared that "If democracy were to meet the challenge of modern society, it had to have traditions of public service powerful enough to enlist the best brains of the country" (170, p. 224). To this end Frankfurter worked for years before realizing some success with the coming of the New Deal.

Jonathan Mitchell credited the rise of professors in the New Deal to a lack of a hereditary land-owning class from which the government could recruit civil servants. The nearest equivalent in the United States to the British Civil Service and the Prussian Beamten were the college professors. In Mitchell's opinion, the professors were like the British and Prussian nobility in that they were above and outside the temptations and preoccupations of the rest of the population. They attained their immunity by virtue of their college posts which established them in the community. In addition, professors are loyal, at least theoretically, to scientific truth and to the scholar's way of

life (139). Lindsay Rogers saw a similar connection: "Because the
federal government has an insufficient number of expert civil servants
comparable to those in Great Britain's administrative class, every
national crisis sees a descent of professors on Washington" (160, p.17).

Continuing with the role of the academician, James V. Forrestal,
Secretary of Defense in the post-World War II era, viewed the administrative expert as an invaluable servant but an impossible master (71,
p. 2). Lippmann viewed the situation in the following manner:

> The real sequence should be one where the disinterested
> expert first finds and formulates the facts for the
> man of action, and later makes what wisdom he can out
> of comparison between the decision, which he understands
> and the facts, which he organized (127, p. 375).

According to Schlesinger, Lippmann favored a partnership between the
expert, who was able to master the material, and the political leader,
who could master the public. In this arrangement the political leader
would act as the intermediary between the experts and his constituency.

The use of experts in government service did not receive unanimous
endorsement. Elihu Root requested the services of academicians when he
served as a cabinet member, but in a letter to Professor George P.
Fisher he outlined the view held by many businessmen and government
officials:

> The great difficulty in the application of pure reason to
> practical affairs is that never in this world does the
> reasoner get all the premises which should affect the con-
> clusions; so it frequently happens that the practical man
> who does not reason at all but who feels the effect of
> conditions which the reasoner overlooks, goes right while
> the superior intelligence of the reasoning man goes wrong
> (143, p. 43).

This position was not predominant and academicians were increasingly pulled into government services as life became more complex in the twentieth century. At least for that part of the twentieth century considered in this study, they appeared to function much more effectively as advisers and resource people than as administrators and possessors of positions of power.

In reviewing the post-Civil War period, it is noteworthy that forces at work in society and higher education had produced or were in the process of producing an atmosphere in which academicians could render a vital service to the nation in addition to their work in the classroom. The flow of academicians to Washington was accelerated by crises such as World War I and the depression following the stock market crash in 1929, but it will be revealed in subsequent chapters that these were peak periods in a continuing trend. The trend was stimulated in the early 1900's by the development of the Progressive Movement and by Theodore Roosevelt's moving into the White House.

CHAPTER III

THE ACADEMICIANS--EARLY NINETEEN HUNDREDS

Leo Gurko asserted that by the opening of the twentieth century poets were no longer being summoned to diplomatic posts and that historians were not being invited to serve in the cabinet (83, p. 107). This statement is valid, at least on the surface, but Gurko did not take into account the changing scope of operation for academicians which was in the making in the area of public service. Academicians reacted positively to the charges against them which were discussed in the previous chapter. Chapter III deals with the academician in government service during the period generally referred to as the Progressive Era. It includes the presidential administrations of Theodore Roosevelt and William Howard Taft and the pre-war years of Wilson's administration. Emphasis is placed on the individuals involved in public service and on the factors that contributed to the emergence of the public service concept. Examples at the state level will be followed by the development of the movement at the national level.

The success of the service ideal can be attributed in part to the conditions in the country at the time the service concept was developing. In the years between the Spanish-American War and World War I, when progressivism was filling the land, universities in the United States achieved significant popular status. The spread of progressivism

43

and the university idea simultaneously tended to reinforce the service element of both (166, pp. 356-57). Timing is also significant when the characteristics of the closing years of the nineteenth century are contrasted with the hope of progressivism. In this regard Rudolph declared: "After the long decades of free-wheeling, atomistic individualism which characterized nineteenth-century America, the appearance of a movement for which service was a touchstone was of considerable importance to higher education"(166, p. 358).

Progressivism

Technological changes that accompanied the coming of the new century had a significant influence on the way people thought and lived. Change was not confined to technology alone, it touched almost all aspects of life. Perhaps the most basic change as far as this study is concerned was the shift in attitudes held about man and his relation to society and to the universe (143, p. 16). Concern for man and improvements in social, political, and economic conditions characterized progressives and opened the door wider for academicians.

One of the unique features of progressivism was that it was manifest in both government and education. The political philosophy of progressivism was partially based on the Jeffersonian concept of education (148, p. 157). As a result progressive leaders in government and education agreed that more democracy would cure what little was wrong with American democracy. Progressives in educations generally supported the basic position of the utility advocates in higher education, but other progressives favored a broader scope. John Dewey thought that a democracy could not flourish where narrow utilitarian education existed for one class and broad liberal education was provided for another (43, p. 125). The question of priorities in the curriculum was not answered, as has been the case in most periods in the development of higher education, but Dewey and other progressives in higher education contributed to the atmosphere that encouraged public service. Perhaps their greatest achievements were helping to remove the mutual distrust between academicians and the rest of society, and promoting intellectual and social progress by putting their knowledge to work to reform society (113, p. 457).

Educational progressives as well as the pragmatists often tended to appear highly theoretical in presenting their practical views. In this regard, Veysey suggested that by the turn of the century, when utility-minded university educators were seeking to up-date their aims, they did not grasp at pragmatism but at a more available device--the idea of efficiency (194, p. 116). Efficiency, which was in keeping with the ideas of public administration and was supported by the social scientist, was at the center of the concept of boards and commissions advocated by the progressives. These progressives in education continued to advance the concept of democratization and in this and in other ways supported progressives in government. It is ironic that the parallel development did not continue. Progressivism as a vital political belief became dormant following the First World War, yet in education it continued to grow even after the War (166, p. 366).

In the early 1900's the estrangement between the academicians and power began to come to an end. A number of factors contributed to the change; perhaps the foremost was the realization that academicians had certain serviceable skills that were becoming increasingly essential to the positive functions of government. The period of what Hofstadter called the "frustrated gentleman" was nearing its end, and the era of the scholar as expert was emerging--thanks partly to progressivism (94, p. 196). As America entered a new phase of economic and social development, there emerged a semblance of balance between the drive for developing industry and occupying the continent and the emphasis placed on humanizing and regulating the large aggregates of power accumulated in the preceding years by industrialists and political bosses. To control and regulate these great powers, it was necessary to reform politics and to build up the administrative system to the point that it could control the economy to some extent (94, p. 197).

Progressivism established the regulatory and administrative agency as a part of government with the introduction of the idea of an expert into what had been a rather uncomplicated concept of the role of government. Trends in this direction caused progressives to turn to universities where experts among the faculty could be found and where others could be trained. Universities were not unaccustomed to this role, since they had begun providing services for the farm and the factory after the Civil War, and especially for agriculture after the passage of the Hatch Act in 1887. The major shift was in the area of specializations as the government began to need people trained in such fields as sociology, political economy, and public adminstration (166, p. 365).

The differences that had existed between democracy and the educated man began to disappear because according to Hofstadter, "The type of man who had always valued expertise was now learning to value democracy and because democracy was learning to value experts" (94, p. 198). More and more academicians were being drawn into political affairs on the basis of usefulness. A new type of professor was also emerging in America. No longer was it possible to dismiss ideas by calling them academic, because the boundary between the academy and society was not seen so clearly as it had been a few years earlier (94, p. 205).

There appeared to be a general recognition of the changes in the status of the professor. Atlantic Monthly indicated in an article in 1902 that a different type of college professor was everywhere in evidence. College professors combined their expertise on bridges, subways, gas commissions, currency, and other technical topics with a practical capacity. They had attained enough status that it was no longer possible to brush them aside contemptuously as mere theorists (35).

Friedrich Poulsen thought by the early 1900's that the American professor had "risen to a very honored position; he is at home in society; he is not a stranger at court either, and he no longer moves in the company of lords with an apologetic air" (185, p. 150).

An article in a 1909 issue of North American Review suggested that it was to the credit of the common sense of the American people that the prejudice against the college professor was decreasing (135). This shift in attitude resulted from the public recognition and appreciation of the service they rendered to the state. The increasing frequency with which their advice was sought in solving the problems of society indicated the extent of appreciation. This appreciation was also due to the public's discovering the improvement in the training of professors and to a growing understanding of the real value of the expert (135).

State use of academicians in public service in the early twentieth century set an example that could be emulated by the national government. In several states, especially in the Mid-west and West, the idea emerged for a state university closely articulated with the life of the people and intimately linked with government. The concept was implemented in varying degrees, and no institution came as close as the University of Wisconsin in epitomizing the spirit of progressivism and the service ideal (166, p. 363). What is generally referred to as the Wisconsin Idea influenced government at the national level, in addition to inspiring reforms in other states. Eric Goldman suggested a direct connection between the Wisconsin Idea and reform efforts in New York, California, New Jersey, Michigan, Iowa, North Carolina, and Texas (79, p. 171). The Wisconsin Idea merits some examination because of its impact and because it embodied much of the progressive spirit.

Wisconsin Idea

Frederick C. Howe, one of the academicians involved with government in Wisconsin, called the Wisconsin Idea "an experiment station in politics, in social and industrial legislation, in democratization of science and higher education." It was, he added, a "statewide laboratory in which popular government is being tested in its reaction on people, on the distribution of wealth, on social well-being" (102, p. vii). Many of these developments were rooted in the history of the state and especially the state university. At the inception of the university the service idea was at least in the germ stage in the Mid-west, and many of its early leaders were service-minded. Carl Schurz was one of the first regents at the University of Wisconsin, and John Bascom, Thomas C. Chamberlain, and Charles K. Adams, all noted leaders in higher education, served as presidents in the last quarter of the nineteenth century. These men were in the forefront of the national trend toward public service. Bascom, an economist, opposed the idea of political economy being a dismal science. To him it was a science through which order, morality, and statemanship could live; it had a moral force (131, p. 21). Chamberlain is credited with stating "Scholarship for the sake of the scholar is simply refined selfishness. Scholarship for the sake of the state and the people is refined patriotism" (28, p. 184).

These men encouraged public service in numerous ways. Extension classes and short courses were offered, agriculture was assisted, new departments were created, and public spirited professors were attracted to Wisconsin. As was generally true across the nation, service took form earliest in agriculture, but the social sciences provided the clearest evidence of affinity with the progressive movement. Notable work was underway in history by the 1880's under the leadership of William F. Allen and Frederick J. Turner. Even more significant was the founding of the School of Economics, Political Science, and History in 1892 under the direction of Richard T. Ely (43, p. 162). In addition to Ely, an economist, the staff included John R. Commons, an expert on labor and industrial questions; E. A. Ross, a sociologist; and Paul S. Reinsch, a political scientist (102, p. 30). These academicians had a tremendous influence on the public service idea, through their writings, classes, and service, on local, state, and national agencies. Their graduate students ultimately served a wide range of agencies as members or advisers.

Robert M. LaFollette's election as governor and the selection of Charles R. Van Hise as university president resulted in the development of an even closer relationship between state government and the university. As a strong supporter of public service, Van Hise viewed the state university's obligation to the state as its first duty. The scope of his thinking regarding public service was indicated in an address to the National Education Association in which he stated: "The field of investigation covers all of the practical problems of the state--agricultural, industrial, political, social, and moral. In short the university aims to become the instrument of the state in its upbuilding -- material, intellectual, and spiritual" (190, p. 70).

Wisconsin became the proving ground for progressivism. Robert M. La Follette and his successors provided the leadership, and the academicians supplied the philosophy of government and the social and economic skills (148, p. 216). It has been argued that the academicians were essential to the growth of the progressive movement. Russel B. Nye stated that the academicians "gave La Follette and other Mid-western progressives a scientific ballast that the.Grangers and Populists lacked, a basis for action without which progressivism could not have successfully developed" (148, p. 148). The extent of university involvement prompted Howe to refer to it as the fourth department of government (102, p. 39). For the 1910-11 school year, Charles McCarthy stated that forty-two professors gave part of their time to the state of Wisconsin (131, p. 313).

The services rendered were almost as numerous as the number of men involved. McCarthy's legislative reference library established in 1901 and the utilization of the idea of expert seem to have had the greatest impact. Mc Carthy made information available to legislators and aided in drafting bills through his library. News of the success of its operation spread, and by 1907 five states had adopted the idea, and by 1917 twenty more such libraries were in existence (148, p. 219). To cope with the problems of labor, finance, social reform, and other complex features of society the state government made extensive use of experts. The use of experts was predicated on the basis that they were trained men familiar with the legislation and literature on current questions in other states and nations (131, p. 139).

The Wisconsin Railway Commission served as an excellent example of how commissions could operate. Commissions in other states had failed because the railroads controlled the members or because there was a lack of men familiar, by education or by experience, with the problems involved. The first chairman of the Wisconsin Commission was B. H. Meyer, who had studied transportation in Germany. Meyer's

service was so creditable that he was subsequently asked to serve on
the United States Interstate Commerce Commission (102, pp. 70-1).
Among the other successful commissions in Wisconsin were the Industrial
Commission and the Tax Commission. The success of the commission at
the state level influenced the creation of similar commissions by the
federal government.

The state of Wisconsin gave academicians their first major opportunity for public service. For the most part they performed well, but
it should be remembered that they were primarily technicians, not policy
advisers (94, p. 202). Their contribution to the state was recognized
by Lincoln Steffens: "What the brain is to a man's hands, feet and eyes,
this university is to the people of the state: the instinctive recourse
for information, light and guidance" (178, p. 363). When La Follette
went to the United States Senate, he took these ideas with him. Through
the union of "soil and seminar," of "brawn and brains," Wisconsin established a precedent that the nation could follow (156, p. 175). The remainder of this chapter will be devoted to the activities of academicians
on the national level.

Presidency of Theodore Roosevelt

Theodore Roosevelt gave an impetus to the trend toward the service
of academicians in government. In Hofstadter's view, "Roosevelt paved
the way for Progressivism by helping to restore prestige to educated
patricians who were interested in reform, by reinvesting their type with

the male virtues." Moreover, Roosevelt dispelled "the image of the gentleman scholar as effeminate and ineffectual in politics. He had begun to show that the gentleman scholar had a useful part to play" (94, p. 196). Some of the time Roosevelt had the air of an academician about him. He had a sound undergraduate background and studied for a short time at the Columbia Law School (142, p. 46). John W. Burgess, one of his professors at Columbia, indicated that Roosevelt was more interested in courses in political history, public law, and political science than in the more restricted area of law. After a short period of time he left law school and was elected to the New York legislature. He continued to serve in various political roles but showed an interest in many other aspects of life. It was his writing in the field of history that he developed the closest association with the academic world.

President Roosevelt called on academicians for advice on railroad control, meat inspection, immigration, and other issues (94, p. 207). In the words of George Mowry, Roosevelt "brought to the public service a host of young, energetic, and educated men from some of the better eastern universities whose like had possibly not been seen in such numbers before" (143, p. 216). All of these men were not academicians but, as will be shown in the following pages, some can be placed in this category. Roosevelt was one of the first presidents to appoint commissions to study selected aspects of American life. Even though most of the staff members were from outside the academic area, the practice contributed to the expanding role for academicians in government service. These study groups needed the expertise possessed by individuals

in higher education, and chief executives after Roosevelt followed his
example by using such commissions. Roosevelt's appraisal of commissions
is indicated by the following statement: "The mere fact that they did
efficient work for the public along lines new to veteran and cynical
politicians of the old type created vehement hostility to them" (162,
p. 402). It is apparent from this statement that Roosevelt recognized
some of the practical problems associated with the use of academicians
and with the entrusting of a commission to study important problems in
the country. Among the most important commissions appointed by Roosevelt were those on Organization of Government Scientific Work, Public
Lands, Inland Waterways, Country Life, and National Conservation (162,
p. 401).

By the time Roosevelt became President, academicians were finding
more opportunities to serve the federal government. Academicians had
been serving in a number of scientific and technical bureaus for several
years. The first Philippine Commission appointed in 1899 by President
McKinley was chaired by Jacob Gould Schurman, president of Cornell University. Schurman completed his work on the first commission; however,
he was prohibited from continuing with the second commission because of
the demands of his position at Cornell (150, pp. 158-9). The second
Philippine Commission, appointed by McKinley in 1900 and headed by
William Howard Taft, was responsible for governing the islands for several years. Of the four members in addition to Taft, two came from university campuses. Dean C. Worcester, also a member of the first commission,
was a zoologist on the faculty of the University of Michigan; he had

gained some familiarity with the Far East from several government-sponsored scientific expeditions. A history professor at the University of California, Bernard Moses, was the other academician. Taft found Moses to be especially helpful in the areas of economics and sociology (150, p. 165).

There were other academicians in government service in the post-Civil War era, as is illustrated by the following examples: Andrew D. White served as minister to Germany from 1879 to 1881; after retiring as president of Cornell, he went to Russia as the minister from the United States (201, p. 476). In the 1890's Professor Thomas C. Mendenhall of the Ohio State University was one of the Bering Sea Commissioners (201, p. 264). Thomas M. Cooley, one of the most renowned professors of law in the country in the late 1800's, helped launch the Interstate Commerce Commission. While teaching at the University of Michigan, he was appointed to the first commission by Cleveland in 1887. It is worthy of note that it was more than two decades before another academician was appointed to the body. This should not be construed as a reflection upon Cooley's record with the Commission. Cooley took the lead in organizing the Commission and then served effectively as a member (90).

It seems ironical that the first person with a Ph. D. degree was elected to Congress in the anti-intellectual era following the Civil War. Henry Cabot Lodge received his doctorate from Harvard in 1876, after having completed undergraduate work and a law degree at the same institution. As a student and later as a faculty member at Harvard, Lodge came under the strong influence of Henry Adams. His association with Adams produced a great interest in reform and caused Lodge to see the need for learned men in politics. Lodge was perhaps more realistic than his mentor because he realized that there was a practical aspect to politics, and he operated within the party organization (77, p. 40). After two terms in the Massachusetts Legislature and active involvement in the Republican Party at all levels, Lodge was elected to the United States House of Representatives in 1886 (7). In 1893 he was elected to the United States Senate, where he served until his death in 1924.

A few federal departments and agencies began to recruit academicians in the post-Civil War period; notable in this regard was the Department of Agriculture. One of the first academicians attracted to Agriculture was Harvey W. Wiley, who became head of the newly created Bureau of Chemistry in 1883 and served in that capacity until 1912. Prior to going to Washington he taught at the Medical College of Northwestern Christian University (now Butler University) in Indiana, and nine years at Purdue University (206, p. 98). He had intended to become a physician but became more interested in chemistry, which led him to a study of food adulteration. Interest in foods was perhaps the major reason he accepted the position in governmental service. While teaching at Purdue he worked with adulterations and noted "tremendous changes had to be brought about before there would be anything like the protection the public needed from impure and dangerous substances" (206, p. 154). He viewed the position with Agriculture as an opportunity to render greater public service than was possible as a college teacher. His most important contribution was probably in connection with the Pure Food and Drug Act.

Wiley was able to bring other academicians into the Department and to enlarge their roles. By the early 1900's, Professors M. A. Scavell and H. A. Weber were serving on a committee with Wiley attempting to develop standards for the purity of foods (206, p. 176). William Frear and A. W. Briting were working fulltime for the Department, and outstanding academicians such as H. H. Rusby and Floyd Robison were serving on a part-time basis (206).

Henry E. Van Deman, first professor of horticulture at Kansas Agriculture College, was attracted to the Department of Agriculture in 1885. He served as the first pomologist and later as head of the Division of Pomology (86, p. 86). Charles William Daliney, Jr., was the second assistant secretary of agriculture from 1894 to 1897. He held a Ph. D. from the University of Göttingen, had taught at several southern universities, and was president of the University of Tennessee when named to the federal position (5, p. 443).

In 1897, President McKinley appointed James F. ("Tama Jim") Wilson, Secretary of Agriculture. Wilson had served in the Iowa legislature and the United States House of Representatives and was professor of agriculture and director of the experiment station at Iowa Agricultural College when he was appointed Secretary of Agriculture (5, p. 40). His tenure spanned the administrations of Presidents McKinley, Roosevelt, and Taft and he contributed greatly to the progress made in the Department during this period (12, p. 119).

It is interesting to observe that academicians seemed to weave in and out of government service for many years, beginning in the early

1900's. This especially characterized the Department of Agriculture, and the same is probably true in other areas but in different degrees. The philosophy and attitude of the higher echelons appeared to influence the extent of involvement. Wilson created a receptive environment for academicians, as indicated in the following statement: "The new Secretary reorganized the Department, brought in a distinguished group of scientists and, in a few years, built up an outstanding research organization" (12, p. 119). Many of the academic people who came into the Department in the early twentieth century remained for several years. Some of these served on a full-time basis, while others were associated with the Department on some type of part-time arrangement.

Wilson's assistant secretary of Agriculture from 1904 to 1913, Willet Martin Hays, had taught at Iowa State College, the University of Minnesota, and North Dakota Agricultural College, where he became known for his work in plant breeding (5, pp. 41, 445). Warner W. Stockberger entered the Department in 1903 as an expert in histology. He had taught at Hanover College (Indiana) and had a Ph. D. degree from George Washington University. In 1908 he was named the Department's pharmacologist, and in 1910 he began to work in plant physiology. Stockberger remained with the Department until 1940 (180, p. 285).

William Jasper Spillman began his long association with the Department in 1901. For the next three decades he moved back and forth between the Department of Agriculture and positions in higher education. As an agronomist in charge of grass and forage plant investigations, he began in 1901 to make a number of surveys or demonstrations (5, p. 43). He was named chief of Farm Management in 1905 and held the position until 1918 (5, p. 102). Following a period of teaching at the University of Missouri, Beverly Thomas Galloway joined the Department and in 1888 he became head of the section of Vegetable Pathology. Various organizational patterns developed in the 1890's, and in 1901 the Bureau of Plant Industry was created to include several areas associated with vegetable research. Galloway headed the Bureau from 1901 to 1913 (5, pp. 43, 460). Wilson utilized the services of an old friend who was in the Department of Agriculture when he became secretary. Seaman A. Knapp had been a professor of agriculture and president of Iowa Agricultural College. He was appointed a statistical agent to report on cotton in 1898. By 1902 he had been appointed special agent in the South. He was responsible for the Department's investigative work and demonstration in the South for several years (5, pp. 43-4).

A real concern for forests in the country began to develop at the national level in the early years of the present century. The roots of national action go back at least to the creation in 1862 of the National Academy of Sciences, which was to assist the government in matters in the field of science. In 1896 a committee of this group made several recommendations concerning forest reserves (51, p. 103). As a result of the recommendations and other factors, the national government took a number of steps regarding the nation's forest. Most of the people associated with forestry in its early stages in the United States were trained in a related field, such as biology, or gained experience on the job. Bernard E. Fernow was chief of the Division of Forestry from 1886 until 1898. Like others in forestry at the turn of the century, Fernow left the Division of Forestry for a teaching position (51, p. 134). For a decade or more men like Fernow and Filibert Roth rotated between the Division of Forestry and some of the new schools of forestry which were established during this period; especially is this true of Roth. The lack of university-trained foresters creates problems in illustrating the involvement of academicians in this aspect of government service. One author suggested that forestry as a profession in the United States dates from the organization of the Society of American Foresters in 1900 (51, p. 275).

Nevertheless, the interest revealed by President Roosevelt and the progressives gave forestry a significant push, and academicians were attracted to this phase of government service in increasing numbers as the years passed. In 1905 the Bureau of Forestry was transferred from the Department of Interior to the Department of Agriculture and was elevated to the Forest Service (51, pp. 114, 144). By the early 1900's two of the academicians in the division were Henry Solon Graves, who served as assistant chief and later Head of the Forest Service, and James W. Toumey, formerly a professor of botany at the University of Arizona (51, p. 136).

The State Department also took advantage of the capabilities possessed by academicians. David Jayne Hill, an excellent scholar with a keen interest in international law, left the presidency of the University of Rochester in 1898 to become assistant secretary of state (182, p. 194). In the years from 1902 to 1911 he served as the American minister to

Switzerland, Sweden, and Holland, and as ambassador to Germany (176, p. 949; 92, p. 245). Roosevelt likewise appointed Maurice Francis Eagan, a witty professor of English at Catholic University, to represent the United States in Denmark (182, p. 220). James Brown Scott left a professorship at the law school of Columbia University to become Solicitor in the State Department. Elihu Root, Secretary of State at the time, indicated to Nicholas Murray Butler that the selection of Scott was one of the most fortunate events of his administration (182, p. 204). Scott's greatest public contribution probably came in connection with the peace settlement after World War I.

W. F. Willoughby, a lecturer at Johns Hopkins and Harvard, served the United States in Puerto Rico from 1901 to 1909. He served as Treasurer of Puerto Rico from 1901 until 1907 and Secretary and President of the Executive Council of the Legislative Assembly from 1907 until 1909 (209, p. 212). Another academician who assisted Roosevelt was John Bassett Moore. Moore began in the State Department in 1885 as a clerk and moved up to third secretary before beginning a teaching assignment in international law and diplomacy at Columbia. He also served as a commissioner at the conference settling the Spanish-American War (141, p. 95). Roosevelt consulted Moore on several foreign problems, and Moore drafted a memorandum on the Panama situation prior to the Panamanian revolt from Colombia (149, pp. 316, 325). Albert W. Shaw, who earned a Ph. D. degree from Johns Hopkins, served Roosevelt as an adviser on Panama and other topics (149, p. 315; 62, p. 278).

An academician whose inclusion in this study is questionable is Nicholas Murray Butler, president of Columbia University. Butler, by his own admission, was acquainted with thirteen Presidents of the United States, and knew seven intimately enough to discuss policy with them (25, p. 10). It appears, however, that his contributions were not of the nature emphasized in this work. Perhaps his greatest connections were through the Republican Party. He served as a delegate to the national convention on more than one occasion, and in 1912 he was the stand-in candidate for Vice President. Vice President Sherman had been renominated but died October 30, 1912, so Butler's name was added to the ballot (151, p. 836). Irving Fisher, the Yale economist, was also on the fringe of the presidential advisors. He discussed monetary and other economic questions with Presidents Theodore Roosevelt, Taft, Wilson, Harding, Hoover, and Franklin D. Roosevelt (168, p. 236), but he did not serve as close adviser to any of the Presidents.

The Industrial Commission was created by Congress in 1898 to investigate questions related to immigration, labor, agriculture, manufacturing, and business and to report to Congress concerning needed legislation (192, p. 518). The Commission used academicians and other experts to collect a fund of highly valuable information which was put in report form and published between 1900 and 1902. John R. Commons began working for the Commission in 1900 by conducting a study on immigration. He then moved to Washington to help write the final report published in 1902. Associating with other experts serving the Commission prompted him to refer to it later as the "first brain trust." In his opinion, it was the first government agency to bring together a staff of trained economists for this purpose (38, p. 76). Following the completion of the work of the Commission, Commons moved back to the classroom. Ely persuaded him to come to Wisconsin, where he continued to render public service.

Edward Dana Durand, who served as secretary to the Industrial Commission from 1900 to 1902, was responsible for retaining most of the experts. He taught at Cornell and Stanford prior to serving the Commission, and after a brief stay at Harvard he returned to government service. After serving in the census office he moved to the Bureau of Corporations, where he was special examiner from 1903 to 1907 (58, p. 177). William Z. Ripley, a prominent economist who taught at Columbia, Massachusetts Institute of Technology, and Harvard, began his association with the federal government by working with the Commission in its early years. Because he was recognized as an expert on transportation, he was engaged to help untangle the relations between the railroads and the anthracite coal industry (157, p. 65).

The man who might be considered the first academician to render a wide range of services to the federal government started with the Industrial Commission. Jeremiah W. Jenks earned a Ph. D. from the University of Halle and held faculty appointments at several of the most prestigious institution in the United States. His initial government service was with the Commission from 1899 to 1901; the next year the War Department engaged him as a special commissioner to the Orient which was followed by a year's service on the Commission on International Exchange. Later he served a three-year term as a member of the United States Immigration Commission. He and Professor W. J. Lauck wrote the final report for the Commission which had been created in 1909 by an act of Congress (107, p. 745). Jenks was the only academician on the Commission, but H. Parker Willis, Franz Boas, and E. A. Goldenweiser conducted studies sponsored by the Immigration Commission (105, p. 571).

The Bureau of Corporations, a part of the Department of Commerce and Labor created in 1903, utilized the services of many academicians. It was primarily responsible for investigating industrial corporations; therefore, experts were needed (192, p. 523). A special examiner for the Bureau from 1904 to 1912 was Francis Walker. As president of Massachusetts Institute of Technology a half-century earlier, Walker's father had advocated public service. The younger Walker taught at Colorado College and Western Reserve University after receiving a Ph. D. degree at Columbia University (196, p. 341).

Scientific and technical agencies of the government also employed academicians in addition to those in the Department of Agriculture. Cleveland Abbe, Jr. entered government service after receiving a Ph.D. degree at Johns Hopkins and teaching for a few years. From 1903 to 1906 he served in the United States Geological Survey and was then transferred to the Weather Bureau, where he remained until 1918 (2, p. 157). Abbe emulated his father at least to a degree in that the elder Abbe had been a college professor before President Cleveland appointed him to the Weather Bureau (6, p. 203).

An academic man who spent most of his working life in government service was George Otis Smith. Like Abbe, Smith earned a doctorate in science from Johns Hopkins University. He joined the Geological Survey in 1901 and was director from 1907 to 1930 (175, p. 385). In 1901 Samuel W. Stratton was appointed the first Director of the Bureau of Standards. Previously he had taught physics and mathematics at the University of Illinois and had been professor of physics at the University of Chicago (181, p. 142). He was joined on the staff of the Bureau of Standards by George K. Burgess in 1903. After receiving a Doctor of Science degree from the University of Paris, Burgess held faculty appointments at the Universities of Michigan and California (23, p. 312).

As the examples during Roosevelt's administration indicate, most of the academicians involved were technicians and experts, but there was greater participation by academicians in all fields; the trend continued to develop during the administrations of Presidents Taft and Wilson.

William Howard Taft's Administration

It may be exaggerating slightly to identify William Howard Taft as an academician, but he did have experience in higher education prior to the twentieth century. In the 1890's he was a federal judge in Cincinnati; and as a result, it was possible for him to accept an offer to teach part-time at his legal alma mater, the University of Cincinnati. In 1896 Taft became dean of the Cincinnati Law School and professor of property; this has to be considered a part-time arrangement, since he only lectured two hours a week (150, p. 125). According to his brother,

Henry, in 1899 the liberal element of the Yale Corporation wanted Taft
to become president of Yale. He declined partly because he did not feel
qualified (150, pp. 44,46). It is not contended here that Taft was an
academician as defined in this study, but the examples cited at least
show a connection with the academic world.

Even though Theodore Roosevelt accused Taft of abandoning the use
of commissions, Taft continued to utilize the services of academicians
in a number of prominent positions (162, p. 402). In 1912 he appointed
a commission of three to study postal rates for magazines and newspapers.
One of the commissioners was A. Lawrence Lowell, president of Harvard
(151, p. 625). The Commission on Efficiency and Economy was appointed
by President Taft in 1911 to study governmental operations in an attempt
to promote efficiency and to reduce cost. Of the six commissioners,
three members, including the chairman, Frederick A. Cleveland, were
academicians.

Frank J. Goodnow, an authority on administrative law and later
president of Johns Hopkins, and William F. Willoughby, who moved from
the Census Bureau, were also on the Commission (151, p. 605). In 1910
Taft nominated Willis Van Devanter to fill a vacancy on the Supreme
Court. Van Devanter had been appointed to a circuit judgeship by
Theodore Roosevelt in 1903. Prior to that he was an assistant attorney
general attached to the Department of Interior and a professor in the
law school at Columbia University, now George Washington University
(202, p. 82).

With "Tama Jim" Wilson continuing as Secretary of Agriculture, the
programs he initiated earlier and the attitudes he represented appear

to have continued. Taft appointed Carl L. Alsberg, a brilliant young biochemist of Harvard, to succeed Wiley as head of the Bureau of Chemistry. Many writers have viewed this as a very progressive step as illustrated by the following statement: "Under his able administration the scientific quality of the Bureau was built up to a high level: its standing in industry and in scientific circles was enhanced" (12, p.151). Alsberg surrounded himself with a number of outstanding scientists; among them were Frederick Belding Power, director of Wellcome Research Laboratory and internationally known for his work in phytochemistry; Claude Silbert Hudson, noted for his work on sugars and carbohydrates; and H. D. Gibbs and E. M. Choce (86, pp. 49-50).

There is no indication that academicians appointed during the Roosevelt years felt uncomfortable because of Taft's policies. In addition to those who remained in the Department, others were added on a full-time basis or as consultants. Kenyon L. Butterfield, president of Rhode Island State College, worked with the Office of Experiment Stations on a proposal that ultimately evolved into the Smith-Lever Act (86, p. 153). Henry Solon Graves, described as the second American to become a professionally trained forester (51, p. 95), was serving as dean of the Yale School of Forestry in 1909 when Gifford Pinchot requested him to serve as chairman of a group to formulate standards for forestry education (51, p. 201). When Pinchot left the Service the following year, Graves was appointed to replace him; he held the position until 1920 (5, p. 458).

E. Dana Durand, who had been in government service since 1900, was appointed Director of the Census Bureau in 1909 (58, p. 177), and W. F.

Willoughby returned from service in Puerto Rico to serve as assistant director (31, p. 1000). Francis Walker was transferred from the Bureau of Corporations to the position of U. S. Deputy Commissioner of Corporations (196, p. 341). David Jayne Hill and Maurice Francis Eagan continued to represent the United States in foreign countries.

The use of experts by the executive and legislative branches continue to grow during the years Taft was in the White House. A Yale professor of economics, Henry C. Emery, served from 1909 to 1913 as chairman of the Tariff Board, which was provided for by the Payne-Aldrich Tariff and was responsible for assimilating information related to tariff questions (63, p. 101). Academicians were also actively involved in the banking and monetary questions during this period.

Balthasar H. Meyer, the first member of a regulatory agency to have an earned doctorate, was appointed to the Interstate Commerce Commission by President Taft. Meyer had ideal credentials for the Commission, at least according to the progressives. After undergraduate work he studied at the University of Berlin, earned a Ph. D. degree at the University of Wisconsin where he remained as a faculty member for a number of years (90, p. 35). Meyer gained practical experience by serving on the Wisconsin Railway Commission before moving to the ICC in 1910. He was reappointed by Presidents Wilson, Coolidge, and Hoover (90, pp. 47,143).

Two academicians from Ohio were elected to Congress in this period. Frank Bartlett Willis had been professor of history and political economy at Ohio Northern University before being elected to the state legislature. He was then elected for two terms in the United States

House of Representatives (207, p. 445). Before his election to the House of Representatives in 1912, Simeon D. Fess had been very active in higher education. At Ohio Normal University he had taught history and had served as dean of the College of Law and vice president. In 1907 he moved to Antioch College, where he became president (67, p. 340). Henry W. Temple, a former professor of history and political science at Washington and Jefferson College, was first elected to the House in 1913. He was elected for a full term in 1915 and continued in the House until 1933 (29, p. 819).

By the end of the first decade of the present century the use of commissions at the state level was well established, and they were becoming increasingly significant on the national level. A discussion of commissions is inserted at this point because of their growing import- ance on the national scene and because of the increasing number of academicians attracted to them. In addition to creating commissions to investigate aspects of national life, the federal government followed the state example and established additional regulatory commissions. Regulation of business affairs by public agencies developed as a reac- tion to the process of industrial and economic change that altered the form of society. Pressure was exerted to create federal regulatory agencies when it became clear that state governments could not provide the desired protection against economic abuses. Advocates of the com- mission idea believed in the expert and in rational solutions to contro- versial regulatory problems. The commission concept was also suggested as a way to insulate the process of governmental regulation of business from partisan politics (167, pp. 9-11).

Commissions flowered at a time when emphasis was placed on efficiency and "scientific" approaches in administration. As has been indicated, both Theodore Roosevelt and Taft appointed commissions to study problems in society, and Taft sponsored the Tariff Commission, which became operational under President Wilson. But the idea of efficiency found its great expression in the increased powers given to the Interstate Commerce Commission and in the creation of the Federal Trade Commission and the Federal Reserve Board. In these the expert became an administrator of policy as well as a gatherer of facts (76, p. 336).

A higher percentage of academicians was found on the commissions than in any other operation of the federal government. Six of the twenty-three tariff commissioners held Ph.D. degrees. From its inception to the mid-1930's, more commissioners on the Interstate Commerce Commission came from higher education than from business (90, pp. 36, 41). E. Pendleton Herring has underscored the nature of the academicians who served as tariff commissioners and "who have been able to turn their academic training to government service with excellent effect" (90, p. 37). Commissions presented academicians with the best opportunity to apply ideas and concepts which they attained through prolonged study.

Not all Americans were convinced that the commission idea would provide the answers to their problems. In the campaign of 1912 Woodrow Wilson lashed out at government by commissions emphasizing the use of experts when he stated:

> What I fear is a government of experts. God forbid that
> in a democratic country we should resign the task and
> give the government over to experts. What are we for
> if we are to be scientifically taken care of by a small
> number of gentlemen who are the only men who understand
> the job. Because if we do not understand the job then
> we are not a free people; we ought to resign our free
> institutions and go to school to somebody and find out
> what it is we are about (119, p. 12).

The irony of this and similar statements is that Wilson was aided in
the campaign by men like Van Hise; that Wilson himself was a professor
of government; that significant new agencies were created at his urging;
and that he brought many men from college and university campuses to
serve as experts and in other capacities(113, p. 12).

Woodrow Wilson and the Pre-War Years

The election of Woodrow Wilson as President of the United States
appeared on the surface to be the ultimate in academicians' influence
on government service. This did not prove to be true; he was not dis-
posed, especially before the war, to make the extensive use of academicians that his background promised (94, p. 209). An understanding of
Wilson's views on public service, briefly described in Chapter II,
helps explain his attitude toward experts. His general governmental
position was unusually aristocratic in the academic milieu of the early
twentieth century (193, p. 630), but by the end of the first decade he
moved toward a more liberal position. The use of academicians in government grew during his administration. A brief description of Wilson's
rise to prominence probably should precede a discussion of his administration. As an undergraduate Wilson was thinking of a political career.

E. M. Hugh-Jones has stated that Wilson studied law because it was the high road to a political career, but that he turned to teaching because of the shortage of clients and his dislike for some of the things that characterized the practice of law and politics (104, pp. 7-8).

Arthur S. Link takes the position that Wilson showed an interest in politics early in his career (122, p. 19). In the 1880's Wilson entered the graduate school at Johns Hopkins, where he completed requirements for the Ph. D. degree in 1886. He taught at Bryn Mawr and Wesleyan University before returning to Princeton, where he had earned a bachelor's degree (104, p. 8). As a scholar he may have reached his peak when his Congressional Government was published in 1885 and was well received (94, p. 208). The success of his first book intensified his desire for an active political career as revealed in a letter to his bride-to-be: "I do feel a very real regret that I have been shut out from my heart's first - primary - ambition and purpose, which was to take an active, if possible a leading part in public life, and strike out for myself, if I had the ability, a statesman's career" (122, p. 19).

After Wilson returned to Princeton as a faculty member, his academic reputation developed rapidly, and he appeared for a time to be more concerned with his status in the profession than in a political career. Whether this was his motive or not, by the early 1900's he was a prominent figure, especially in educational circles. The scope of his reputation is indicated by presidencies offered him by the University of Alabama, Williams College, Washington and Lee, University of Illinois, University of Nebraska, University of Minnesota, and on three occasions the University of Virginia (122, p. 23).

When Wilson was elevated to the presidency of Princeton, he had an additional outlet for his energies; but as time passed and problems compounded, his thoughts again turned to politics. In 1907 Wilson considered running for the United States Senate but even though he had considerable support he decided to remain at Princeton (122, p. 105). By 1910 conditions had changed, and he sought and captured the governorship of New Jersey; then in 1912 he was elected to the Presidency of the United States.

Even though Wilson did not use academicians as extensively as might have been expected, many were brought in prior to the war, and by virtue of his education and actions, academicians felt comfortable during his administration. As David F. Houston aptly pointed out, "With him government was an instrument for public service and ends and not for individual or class profits" (106, p. 16).

Houston was not only the first academician appointed to the Cabinet in this century but the only one to receive such recognition for more than half a century. He served seven years as Wilson's Secretary of Agriculture and the final year of Wilson's administration as Secretary of the Treasury (100). After completing an undergraduate program at the University of South Carolina, he attended Harvard and received the M.A. in political science. At the University of Texas he taught political science and later served as dean of the faculty. Then he became president of the Agricultural and Mechanical College of Texas, served as president of the University of Texas, and was chancellor of Washington University at St. Louis when Wilson asked him to join the cabinet (5, pp. 63, 445).

Houston's association with Wilson had been very limited prior to his cabinet service. Link credits his selection to the strong support of his old friend, Colonel Edward M. House (124, p. 137). Even though Houston was a distinguished economist, he was not widely known as an authority on farm problems, and as a classical economist he opposed direct federal assistance to underprivileged groups (123, p. 30; 124, p. 138). This position made him somewhat of a misfit during the first term of Wilson's administration, but he made significant contributions and brought the Department to a new level of efficiency. Houston states that he had always been interested in public affairs and had studied and lectured on subjects related to government and its problems (100, p. 1). He gave a number of reasons for accepting the invitation to join the cabinet. He viewed the Department of Agriculture as the one great developmental agency of the government. To him the farmers' more acute problems were in the field of economics, a field in which he was interested and one which economists had tended to neglect. Finally, Houston commented, "It was the call which came to head this department under a chief like Mr. Wilson that made me willing to interrupt my work at St. Louis" (100, p. 16).

Houston made use of academicians he found in the Department, brought in others and frequently consulted with his former associates, especially those from the land-grant colleges (5, p. 64). The Department had indicated some interest in agricultural economics prior to the new administration, but in 1913 the Bureau of Markets was established and given responsibility for this vital area (12, p. 137). After the War the work came to fruition under Houston's leadership. Thomas N. Carver, professor of economics at Harvard, was frequently consulted by Houston. Carver was part of the group composed of men outside the Department who assisted in the departmental reorganization in 1913. With the inception of the Rural Organization Service in 1913, which was an outgrowth of Roosevelt's Country Life Commission, Carver was appointed to supervise its work (5, pp. 64, 74). Beverly T. Galloway, an academician who had worked in the Department since 1888, served as assistant secretary from March 1913 to July 1914; when he resigned to become dean of the New York State College of Agriculture (5, p. 67). Galloway was most effective as assistant secretary and played a vital role in the reorganization of the Department (5, pp. 64-69).

A minor argument could be presented in regard to the certifying of Wilson's attorney general as an academician. James C. McReynolds practiced law in Nashville, Tennessee, after graduating from Vanderbilt Law School. He had served as assistant attorney general from 1903 to 1907 and assisted in the prosecution of the American Tobacco Company beginning in 1910 (124, p. 116). His role as an academician was on a part-time basis and not of the same importance as most of the others included in the study.

Academicians were brought into the State Department in increasing numbers. Wilson wanted the eminent authority on international law, John Bassett Moore of Columbia, for the most important office under the Secretary, that of Counselor. Moore finally accepted but served in the position for only eleven months (124, p. 98). Albert H. Putney, dean

of the Illinois College of Law, was appointed head of the Division of
Near Eastern Affairs (124, p. 98). Other academicians represented the
United States abroad. Paul S. Reinsch, head of the Department of Political Science at the University of Wisconsin, was named minister to
China. A professor of English literature at Princeton and a friend of
Wilson's, Henry Van Dyke, became minister to the Netherlands (182, p.
228). Jacob Gould Schurman, president of Cornell and chairman of the
first Philippine Commission, represented the United States in Athens
(182, p. 263). Wilson offered appointments in the Foreign Service to
two other academicians but they declined. Charles W. Eliot was offered
the position of minister to China in 1913 and later the ambassadorship
to Great Britian but rejected each offer (124, pp. 98-9). Wilson wanted to appoint his friend Henry B. Fine, mathematics professor at Princeton, ambassador to Germany but Fine could not afford the position (124,
p. 101).

Frederic C. Howe made his debut in federal service under Wilson
as commissioner of Immigration at Ellis Island (169, p. 43). Howe had
earned his Ph. D. degree at Johns Hopkins under Richard Ely and after-
wards taught at Wisconsin and served as an expert in several progressive
administrations at both state and local levels (148, p.202). Charles
D. Mahaffie, a Rhodes Scholar and professor of jurisprudence at Princeton, began his period of government service in 1916 as a solicitor in
the Department of Interior (90, p. 64). Wilson also brought William Z.
Ripley back into government service by appointing him to a commission
responsible for reporting on the Adamson Act (157, p. 65). All of these
men played important roles in government in the years that followed.

Academicians continued to exert their influence as they worked with the boards and commissions in the early 1900's. They were probably most conspicuous in connection with the monetary and banking questions of the early 1900's. The National Monetary Commission created by the Aldrich-Vreeland Act of 1908 was composed of Congressmen, but they consulted with academicians. J. Lawrence Laughlin, a conservative economist at the University of Chicago, was frequently contacted for advice by Senator Nelson W. Aldrich, the chairman of the Commission (117, pp. 4, 16). The commission also published a number of monographs which were prepared primarily by academicians. The authors were J. T. Holdsworth of the University of Pittsburgh, Davis R. Dewey of the Massachusetts Institute of Technology, O. M. W. Sprague of Harvard, David Kinley of the University of Illinois, Edwin W. Kemmerer of Cornell, and Joseph French Johnson of New York University (117, p. 281).

H. Parker Willis also began his long period of association with the federal government in the early 1900's. Willis had earned the Ph. D. degree at the University of Chicago under the direction of Laughlin. From 1898 to 1905 he taught at Washington and Lee and then took up journalism (117, p. 105). As a graduate student, professor, and journalist, he established himself as an authority in the areas associated with the monetary question. As a result the House Ways and Means Committee engaged him as an expert adviser, and when Carter Glass began the search for an expert to help frame the new bank bill, Willis got the appointment (208, p. 294; 117, p. 105). Willis appears to have contributed more than the other experts in drafting the Federal Reserve Act; however, others submitted drafts and suggestions. Notable in this regard

were Laughlin and a fellow-student of Willis's at Chicago, William A.
Scott, who held a professorship at the University of Wisconsin (117,
pp. 110-12).

When the Federal Reserve Board was created, Willis was appointed
its first secretary (123, p. 45). Of the four original commissioners,
one, Adolph C. Miller, was an academician. Miller had taught at Harvard, Cornell, and Chicago; and from 1902 to 1913 was a professor of
economics at the University of California. He then became assistant
to the Secretary of the Interior for a year, following which he was appointed to the Federal Reserve Board (90, p. 119). The Federal Reserve
gave academicians an additional opportunity for service. In fact, John
R. Commons considered it the first permanent branch of the federal government to have a trained staff of economic investigators (38, p. 76).

Congress created the Industrial Relations Commission in August,
1912, but the Senate refused to confirm Taft's nominations to the I.R.C.;
therefore, President Wilson named the commissioners (192, p. 531).
John R. Commons declined the chairmanship but agreed to serve on the Commission (38, p. 166). Since the Commission was created to study labor
problems, it required the services of a number of capable investigators.
Among the more prominent academicians involved were George E. Barnett of
The Johns Hopkins University, D. A. McCabe of Princeton, and Robert F.
Hoxie of the University of Chicago (38, p. 167; 103, p. 415).

The passage of the act in 1914 creating the Federal Trade Commission
also provided a potential for government service. The act terminated the
Bureau of Corporations and transferred its investigative powers to the

new commission (192, p. 535). As a result the Commission had a broad scope of operation and needed the services of experts. Although not one of the original commissioners was an academician, Francis Walker became chief economist for the body and served in that capacity until 1941 (196, p. 341).

As has been indicated, the Tariff Commission made extensive use of academicians. Academicians on the early commission were Frank W. Taussig and W. S. Culbertson (90, p. 131). Taussig, an economics professor at Harvard, was also named chairman by Wilson and asked to organize the Commission and start it on its way. His selection was based on his reputation as an outstanding economist and an acknowledged authority on the tariff (90, p. 116). Culbertson received a Ph. D. degree from the University of Berlin in 1911, following which he worked for the Tariff Board and the Federal Trade Commission. In 1917 Wilson appointed him to the Tariff Commission (29, p. 187).

Wilson appointed Winthrop M. Daniels, a former professor of economics at Princeton, to the Interstate Commerce Commission in 1914. Earlier as governor he had named Daniels to the New Jersey Board of Public Utility Commissioners (124, p. 449).

The gains made up to World War I by academicians desiring to provide government service are apparent. However, these gains were small compared with the opportunities created as a result of the involvement of the United States in World War I.

CHAPTER IV

THE ACADEMICIANS-WORLD WAR I AND THE TWENTIES

The War Effort

World War I was the most influential factor up to that time in
the history of the United States in drawing academicians into government service. This chapter deals with what are generally considered
the low point (the twenties) and one of the peak periods (World War I)
in public service in this century. Chronologically it covers the span
of time from the involvement of the United States in the war through
Herbert Hoover's administration. Contrary to the opinions of some,
the period of the twenties is viewed as something other than a barren
decade as far as the public service-oriented academicians are concerned.

The number of academicians involved in the many aspects of World
War I was so enormous that only a small percentage of the total number
is included. George Creel's statement that he had no less than "2,500
head" of historians on his list to help the Committee of Public Information illustrates the problem faced, even after one considers that the
number was probably padded (81, p. 423). Claude C. Bowman reinforced
this position by declaring that a separate listing of professorial
activities would be an almost interminable task (16, p. 148). Therefore,
an effort has been made to mention only those who served in the more
responsible areas, to include statements made at the time about the
scope of service, and to note briefly the influence of the war on the

concept of public service. A list of academicians associated with the war effort, but not discussed in the body of this chapter, is included in the appendix.

While higher education in the United States was influenced in a number of ways by World War I, the concern here is primarily with regard to governmental personnel. When the United States entered the war, the government instinctively turned to the colleges and universities for the elemental qualities which would produce manpower (110, p. 79). The better literary magazines of the time frequently carried articles on the relationship between the war and higher education. Scribner's published an article declaring that officers of government, civil and military, immediately appealed to the colleges for leadership when war was declared. The article further suggested:

> In every section of the country representatives of the military, the Red Cross, the Department of Agriculture, called into conference college executives and laid before them the dependence of the government in the emergency upon her best-equipped sons. College men had the training of body and mind and conscience (110, p. 79).

The following statement from a magazine article published in the early twenties reflected a similar view: "A great many of our best teachers particularly college teachers, were utilized in war work -- not only teachers of applied science, but teachers of history, economics, and languages. These men almost always did extremely well" (84, p. 15). Academicians served in Military Intelligence, Chemical Welfare, the Department of State, the War Industries Board, the Ordinance Department, the Committee on Public Information, and in numerous

other capacities (78, p. 466); this list indicates that the selection
was not limited to one specialized area, but that academicians were engaged from practically all disciplines.

Claude C. Bowman analyzed articles concerning college professors
published in general magazines from 1890 to 1938 and drew the following
conclusions concerning their war effort:

> Professors worked out the system of intelligence tests,
> compounded poisonous gases and devised gas masks, organ-
> ized schools for the training of fliers, and invented
> codes for the communication of military secrets. Other
> professors plotted the commerce of the world, studied
> Germany closely, mobilized the youth of the country,
> converting colleges into army camps (16, p. 148).

In turning to the quantitative aspect briefly, we find that the
response was large. One account indicated the following contribution
to the war effort: Princeton sent 40 of its faculty, while 50 went from
the University of Chicago and 50 from Northwestern; Colorado provided the
war with 54 faculty, the University of Louisville with 50, Yale with 40,
University of Wisconsin with 74 (110, p. 81). Of course, this is just
a portion of a lengthy list. President Van Hise of the University of
Wisconsin stated that the war effort of his institution was exceptional
but still typical of the higher educational institutions of the country.
The faculty asked that a leave of absence be granted without prejudice
to rank and seniority to a faculty member performing public service service for national defense. According to Van Hise, of the men on the
faculty of the University of Wisconsin at the outbreak of the war to
June 10, 1918, one hundred and eighty-seven were on leave of absence devoting their full energy to war work (191, pp. 67-8).

The American war propaganda arm, the Committee on Public Information, utilized the services of many prominent academicians, especially
from the field of history. Some served on a full-time basis, and others
contributed their talents but maintained their faculty status. George
Creel headed the committee with subordinates in charge of selected areas.
Production was placed under the jurisdiction of Guy Stanton Ford, head
of the history department at the University of Minnesota. He was
assisted by 23 well-known professors from 15 of the more prestigious
schools in the nation (81, p. 421).

Other historians worked through the National Board for Historical
Service headed by James T. Shotwell of Columbia University. Shotwell
was aided by sixteen professors, the majority of whom were not with
Ford's group (81, p. 423). Academicians were also active in other
areas of propaganda, such as the distribution of information. Some
served in this capacity as civilians, while others joined a branch of
one of the services, frequently with the rank of an officer.

Academicians were often associated with the multitude of boards and
agencies created by the government in mobilizing for war. William Z.
Ripley, the transportation expert at Harvard, was administrator of labor
standards for the War Department and later chairman of the national adjustment committee of the Shipping Board (157, p. 66). Taussig combined
his work on the Tariff Commission with service on numerous boards (144,
pp. 179, 362).

The dean of the graduate school of business administration of Harvard, Edwin F. Gay, served with the Shipping Board, the War Industries

Board, and other agencies (29, p. 296). Leonard P. Ayres used his training in economics and statistics in serving the War Industries Board and other agencies. He had a Ph.D. degree from Boston University in 1910 and worked with the Russell Sage Foundation for the next decade in addition to lecturing at several universities (29, p. 30).

The Food Administration, headed by Herbert Hoover, attracted many academicians. Hoover appointed Ray Lyman Wilbur, president of Stanford, Chief of the Administration's Conservation Division (85, p. 53). Olin Templin, dean of the College of Liberal Arts and Sciences at the University of Kansas became director of School and College Activities within the Conservation Division. Charles Van Hise and F. C. Woodward, two well-known academicians, also served in the Division (144, p. 358). The President's Fair Wheat Price Committee include four academicians. In addition to Taussig there were three college presidents: Harry A. Garfield of Williams College, Edwin F. Ladd of North Dakota Agricultural College, and Henry J. Walters of Kansas State Agricultural College (144, p. 361). Charles McCarthy of Wisconsin fame, Jacob G. Schurman of Cornell, and Albert N. Merritt were among those available to the Commission (144, pp. 360, 365). Merritt had received a doctorate in political economy and political science from the University of Chicago and later earned a law degree; he taught for a brief period before entering business and went to Washington in 1917 to serve the Food Administration (138, p. 214).

There are other areas in which academicians made noteworthy contributions. The first significant service to government by psychologists was rendered in this period. In 1917 Robert Yerkes, president of the American Psychological Association, offered the services of the Association to construct group intelligence tests (43, p. 187). The academicians listed in connection with the war are only representative of the total group.

The war did more perhaps than any other single factor to change the image of the American college professor. One journalist stated: "The professor can no longer be regarded as a species of harmless animal life. The gulf between the theoretical and the practical has been effectively bridged by the fact that the government turns to school laboratories and technicians in its hour of need" (110, p. 82).

An article in Scribner's, written by a former army captain, reflected a similar view. He credited professors with fighting in the war and managing affairs in such a manner that they refuted the ancient and libellous idea that they constituted an absent-minded third sex (78, p. 465). He declared that the professor had done a remarkably large number of different things and had done most of them successfully. Finally, the professor "has proved himself a leader and executive as well as an investigator, which is precisely where the element of surprise comes in. Moreover, he has cooperated, not to say competed, with other men drawn from almost every business and profession" (78, p. 466).

Another effect of the war and the ensuing peace was the impetus given to the academicians in the social sciences. Economists were needed during the war to advise on financing, allocation of resources, production, transportation, labor and consumption; and when it came to

making peace their advice was needed on war debts, reparations, taxation, and reconstruction (46, p. 71). Political scientists were also
used more widely during the war. This acceleration began with the
creation of boards and agencies prior to the war and multiplied with
the increase in government employment and regulation associated with
the war (46, p. 73). When the guns fell silent there was not an immediate exodus of academicians from the positions they had held during
the war. Many remained to assist in demobilization, and academicians
provided a vital service in the making of the peace. Still others
elected to stay in the government service on a long-range basis.

Making the Peace

Approximately five months after the United States entered the war,
Colonel House, at the request of President Wilson, began to enlist a
body of academicians to collect and collate information that might be
needed in the peace conference (99, p. 1). Wilson felt that such a
group was needed because the policy of isolation and the lack of size-
able permanent staffs in most departments resulted in a shortage of
people conversant, through travel and trade, with the interrelations
and internal composition of the nations in Europe and Asia and their
dependents. The group was to attract as little publicity as possible
as indicated by its name--"Inquiry" (99, pp. 1, 3).

All of the academicians associated with the Inquiry and the Peace
Conference are not included. Hofstader stated that at one time the
Inquiry included as many as 150 (94, p. 212), many of whom could be

considered academicians. Those who were responsible for a particular area or otherwise played a significant role are included. When Wilson asked Colonel House to bring a group of academicians together, House turned to Sidney E. Mezes, president of City College of New York. Mezes, who happened to be House's brother-in-law, was named director of the Inquiry and given the responsibility for its organization. Mezes had been president of the University of Texas before moving to New York, and had been familiar with the political currents in the Southwest. Therefore, he was a natural choice because of his connections and especially since he would be working with a large number of univeristy personnel (172, pp. 4-5).

There seems to be some uncertainty about the objectives of the Inquiry as illustrated by William E. Dodd, the University of Chicago history professor. The instructions and assignments given to Dodd and some of the others were frequently changed in the early months of the Inquiry (50, pp. 95-8). As it developed the Inquiry's two main tasks were the "delimitation of its field of work and the selection and training of its personnel" (99, p.2). The personnel include many of the nation's most respected scholars. James T. Shotwell, professor of history at Columbia, was asked to assist in securing the services of associates in history, geography, and economics; and later he headed the division of history (172, p. 5; 31, p. 998). Archibald C. Coolidge of Harvard was one of the first additions. He was recognized in America as an authority on the history of Eastern Europe and as a master of the literature of European diplomatic history (172, p. 6).

Since geography would be of extreme importance, Isaiah Bowman, director of the American Geographical Society, was invited to join the Inquiry. Prior to this he had held faculty positions at Yale, Harvard, and Michigan State, and later became president of The Johns Hopkins University (29, p. 87; 172, p. 6). Anglo-American relations, colonial policy, and certain economic questions were assigned to George L. Beer of Columbia (172, p. 7). Allyn A. Young of Cornell was head of the division of economics; Charles H. Haskins, dean of the Harvard Graduate School, was responsible for the eastern frontier of France; and the Harvard historian, Robert H. Lord, was given the problems of Poland (172, p. 8). Problems of Austria-Hungary were assigned to Charles Seymour of Yale; Clive Day, also of Yale, was given the Balkans. W. E. Lunt of Haverford College studied the historical background of Italian boundary claims (172, p. 9).

Dana C. Munro of Princeton and W. L. Westermann of Cornell dealt with the problems connected with Turkey and the Far East, while Douglas Johnson of Columbia made geographic studies of the Adriatic area. Stanley K. Hornbeck, from the University of Wisconsin, was in charge of the thorny problem of China and Japan; and Mark Jefferson of Michigan State Normal College at Ypsilanti served as chief cartographer (99, p. 7; 172, p. 9). James Brown Scott, previously cited for his years in the State Department, served as judge advocate during the war and was assigned to the international law division of the Inquiry. Scott had taught at a number of universities in the United States in addition to performing numerous services for the government (29, p. 738; 99, p. 7).

Shotwell said that the breadth of Scott's scholarship and his experience, mainly through international conferences, was unique in the United States except for Elihu Root (172, p. 10). Among the other academicians associated with the Inquiry were Frank M. Anderson, Dartmouth; Parker T. Moon, Columbia; and Preston W. Slosson, Columbia. (172, p. 9).

In 1918 the Inquiry made an outline report which Wilson used in formulating the Fourteen Points (99, p. 2). Following this many members of the Inquiry found themselves in Paris. Shortly afterward it was practically dissolved as an organization and renamed the Territorial Section of the Peace Conference (99, p. 6). Most of those previously mentioned went to Versailles, and only minimal assignment changes were made. Among the other noted academicians to assist in the conference were Amos S. Hershey, Wallace Notestein, and Manley Hudson (172, pp. 32, 129, 139). The Central Bureau of Planning and Statistics, organized in Washington in 1918 under Edwin F. Gay, included a number of academicians with training in statistics and economics (172, p. 421). Some of this number and others with similar training went to Versailles to assist in making the treaty. Included in the number were Leonard P. Ayres, a Colonel in the Army; Leo Wolman, a Hopkins professor; and H. Parker Willis (29, p. 911; 172, p. 421; 207, p. 294). Perhaps one of the most scholarly men among the Americans associated with the Peace Conference was Roland B. Dixon. Dixon earned a Ph. D. degree at Harvard and became a member of the faculty. By 1912 he was a professor of anthropology and curator of ethnology of the Peabody Museum of Archaeology and Ethnology at Harvard. He later served as ethnographer to the American commission and as an expert on Inner Asia (56, pp. 237-38).

Colleges and universities had never had an opportunity for service equal to the making of the peace, unless it was during the war. Academicians were not at the top levels of negotiations, but they were concerned with the delicate questions of policy, and their decisions frequently remained intact after being reviewed by the Supreme Council (99, p. 8). Shotwell noted that the pressure at the conference brought academicians into the work of the Inter-Allied Commissions where they helped shape the Treaty (99, p. 16). Academicians enhanced their reputations through their work with the peace, as they had done during the war; however, as will be shown later, the peace effort had an adverse affect on the utilization of academicians in public service.

On the domestic scene academicians continued to provide vital services. The regulatory commissions and other government organizations continued to utilize the services of the trained expert. A few examples are cited to offer support for this contention. William Z. Ripley, the transportation expert, worked with the Interstate Commerce Commission from 1920 to 1923 as a special examiner (157, p. 66). The Tariff Commission found academicians most helpful in this period. Wilson appointed Thomas W. Page, a respected academician, to the Commission in 1918. Page had earned a Ph. D. degree at Leipzig and had attended Oxford and the University of Paris after completing undergraduate work at the University of Virginia. He had taught and served as an administrator at the Universities of California and Texas and had served on Taft's Tariff Board and several other boards during the war (90, pp. 62, 116). Among the experts working for the Commission were Lindsey Rogers, from the

University of Virginia (31, p. 996); Abraham Berglund, who left a teaching position at the University of Washington; and Henry Chalmers, who earned a doctorate at Cornell in 1914 (29, pp. 61, 141).

Roy G. Blakey of the University of Minnesota was brought into the Treasury as assistant director of the savings division (29, p. 72). Ernest L. Bogart of the University of Illinois served as a regional economist in the foreign trade adviser's office in the Department of State (31, p. 988). Wilson made a recess appointment to the Inter-state Commerce Commission in 1920, which the Senate failed to confirm because of the time element; nevertheless, Henry J. Ford, a professor of government and friend of Wilson, served on the Commission for a few months.

One of the most significant areas of development in the closing years of Wilson's administration was in the Department of Agriculture. Elmer Darwin Ball, vice president of Utah Agricultural College, was named assistant secretary with less than a year of Wilson's term re-maining; however, Ball, like many others, remained after Wilson left office (5, p. 442). George Irving Christie of Purdue and President Raymond Allen Pearson of Iowa State College served as special assist-ant secretaries during the war. These examples are indicative of the trend taking place in the Department of Agriculture (5, pp. 67, 448). Impressive was the fact that the Department attracted prominent aca-demicians like Ball whom it held, and others like Pearson, who left to become president of the University of Maryland but continued to serve as an adviser to the department (5, p. 448).

Another development of importance in the department was the movement to study agricultural economics. By 1913 the bureaus of Plant Industry and Markets were being encouraged to work in the area. Perhaps more important in the long run was the work that academicians outside the Department were doing since they were soon drawn into the Department. Leaders in the field were Henry C. Taylor of Wisconsin, George F. Warren of Cornell, Willet M. Hayes and Andrew Boss of Minnesota, Thomas N. Carver of Harvard, and William J. Spillman of the USDA (12, p. 137).

In 1918 a report regarding the proper place of economics in the Department was submitted to Secretary Houston by a committee of academicians composed of Christie; William M. Jardine, president of Kansas State Agricultural College and later Secretary of Agriculture; and B. H. Hibbard, agricultural economist at the University of Wisconsin (5, p. 93). Within a few months one of the nation's authorities in agricultural economics, Henry C. Taylor, was brought to Washington as chief of the Office of Farm Management (5, p. 93). As head of the Department of Agricultural Economics at the University of Wisconsin, he had trained a number of outstanding graduates (12, p. 205).

In 1905 Taylor published the first textbook on agricultural economics (149, p. 194). He was soon joined by his colleague from Wisconsin, Lewis C. Gray, and a former faculty member at Wisconsin, Oliver E. Baker, who had been in the department since 1912 (29, p. 35; 62, p. 191). The Bureau of Agricultural Economics was created in 1921; however, this and other aspects of the department will be discussed later (5, p. 107).

The Twenties

When Wilson vacated the White House in 1921, a significant number of academicians were engaged in government service. The war, an academician in the White House, the Progressive Movement, and other factors contributed to the increase in the number during the early years of the century. However, the point that should be given emphasis at this juncture is that by the opening of the twenties, there were academicians in vital governmental positions who elected to remain. The number attracted to government service in the twenties was not as large as it had been in the later years of the second decade, but many of those who had selected government positions became career employees. It seems that a very important fact is overlooked in dealing with the twenties, and that is that academicians were serving in many facets of government when the decade opened and that others were added prior to the inauguration of Franklin D. Roosevelt.

Certainly the period from 1921 to the early thirties is not characterized by a mass movement of academicians into government service. The attitudes of those at the upper echelons of government were not as encouraging as they had been in the previous decade. The fading of the Progressive Movement in the twenties adversely affected the service role of academicians because the public service idea had developed somewhat parallel to the Progressive Movement. Hugh-Jones noted a difference in the Progressive Movement in the second and third decades of this century: "There is the steady drive of the progressive movement through the presidencies of Theodore Roosevelt, Taft, and Wilson until the youthful enthusiasm becomes pale and spectre-thin and dies in the Republican era of the nineteen-twenties" (104, p. 54). Even though J. Stanley Lemons and others contend that progressivism continued through the decade of the twenties, there seems to be little question that it declined considerably (118).

In attempting to assess the position of academicians at this period, it seems appropriate to note that their use at the state level had been firmly established. Albert W. Atwood supported this contention in an article written in 1933: "Professors of various kinds--especially those associated with state universities--have come to permeate in an utterly prosaic sort of way the agricultural, industrial, governmental, and fiscal affairs of the various states all without attracting the least notice" (4, p. 89).

The attitudes and outlooks of academicians at the beginning of the twenties are difficult to assess. Many involved in the war and in the peace were disappointed with the settlement and perhaps felt guilty and ashamed (94, p. 213). One writer thought they "entertained fervid expectations of triumph and reform as a result of the war and were disappointed by the compromise peace at the end" (50, p. 123). Those who took such a position seemed to establish the credo of no more dashes into the political jungle (50, p. 124). Such a position was not unanimous, but it seemed to be the strongest position for a few years. In fact many academicians appeared to have hastily retreated to their ivory towers in the twenties. Looking at one group of academicians from his vantage point in 1940, Chester C. Davis was critical of this attitude:

"Most of the farm economists sat through the yeasty decade from 1921 on like Buddhas contemplating their respective navels. For years after the post-war crisis had shaken the American farmer's world, the great land grant colleges and their economic staffs remained stodgily unconcerned"(53, p. 3). This colorful statement could undoubtedly have applied to many academicians, but this study is concerned with those who took the opposite attitude, and there were many.

Administrations of Harding and Coolidge

Since Warren G. Harding was President for only a little more than two years, the Harding and Coolidge administrations are discussed in the same section. Of the seven men who occupied the highest governmental office in the country during the scope of this study, Harding and Coolidge had the least in common with academicians. However, they did not completely turn their backs on academicians in government service.

The Department of Agriculture continued to attract and hold academicians. Henry C. Wallace became secretary when Harding's Cabinet was sworn in and served until his death on October 25, 1924. He was known mainly as an agricultural journalist; but before joining the family paper, Wallace's Farmer, he taught dairying at Iowa State College (5, p. 450). His successor, William M. Jardine, had a lengthy association with the academic world as well as some connections with the Department. He had been on the faculties of Utah State Agricultural College and Kansas State Agricultural College. In addition to teaching he had been dean of agriculture, director of the agricultural experiment station, and president of Kansas State Agricultural College. He had served the Department of Agriculture on at least two occasions before becoming its secretary. From 1907 to 1910 he was in charge of dry land grain investigations, and in 1918 he served on a committee studying the proper field of work for the Office of Farm Management (5, pp. 92, 125, 446).

William J. Spillman was brought back to the Department in 1922 after being associated with it in the early years of the twentieth century (5, p. 102). Shortly after Wallace became secretary, Elmer D. Ball, who had been assistant secretary since June 1920, was appointed director of Scientific Work and concurrently served as director of the Department's newly formed Graduate School (5, pp. 103, 113). Ball is a prime example of the academicians who came into government service prior to the twenties and remained through much or all of that decade. A former teacher and agricultural journalist, Charles W. Pugsly, became assistant secretary after Ball. Pugsley had taught agriculture at the University of Nebraska and was director of extension work before becoming editor of the Nebraska Farm. He was assistant secretary from October, 1921, to September, 1923 (5, p. 449). In 1925 Ball relinquished the directorship of Scientific Work to Albert F. Woods of the Bureau of Plant Industry. Prior to joining the Department, Woods had been dean of Minnesota State Agricultural College and president of the University of Maryland (5, p. 224).

In July, 1923, the Department took another step that was destined to increase its need for academicians. The Bureau of Home Economics was established, with Louise Stanley as its chief. She came to the position from the University of Missouri, where she had been chairman of the

Home Economics Division (5, p. 106). From 1924 to 1935 Hildegarde Kneeland was chief of the Bureau. She had held faculty appointments at Vassar, Barnard College, Missouri, and Kansas State Agricultural College before taking a position with the government (29, p. 457). When the Office of Information was created by the Department of Agriculture in 1925, Nelson A. Crawford, head of the Industrial Journalism Department of Kansas State College, was named director (5, p. 126). He appointed a colleague, Samuel Pickard, chief of the Radio Service (5, p. 127).

The number of academicians who made government service a career appeared to be on the upswing in the twenties, especially in agriculture. Mordecai Ezekiel, who is representative of this group, began working for the Department of Agriculture during Harding's administration before he received a doctorate. By 1926 he had a Ph. D. degree and by the early thirties was playing a significant part in departmental activities (29, p. 254; 170, p. 215). Another example of the career man was John B. Hutson. After completing undergraduate work at Western Kentucky State Normal School and the University of Kentucky, he earned a master's degree and a doctorate at the Universities of Wisconsin and Columbia, respectively. He began his career with the Department in the Office of Farm Management and worked in several areas before becoming undersecretary in 1945 (5, p. 446).

The Department continued to utilize the services of academicians as consultants. Among those to serve in such a capacity were George F. Warren of Cornell, who aided in the reorganization in the Bureau of

Markets and Crop estimates, and Carroll Doten of the Massachusetts Institute of Technology (5, p. 107). The recently created Bureau of Agricultural Economics also added a number of academicians in the twenties. Among the number were George B. L. Arner, formerly of Dartmouth; Robert S. Fletcher of Massachusetts Institute of Technology; Lewis E. Long from Louisiana; Paul L. Miller of the University of Minnesota; and Frederick V.Waugh, who had earned a Ph. D. degree from Columbia in 1929 (29, pp. 24, 271, 504, 573, 873).

Committees composed of prominent Americans and assigned a particular problem to study were not used extensively by Harding or Coolidge. Coolidge did appoint one such group in 1924 to study agricultural conditions and to recommend legislation. Of the original membership of nine, two were academicians: W. C. Coffey, dean of the Minnesota College of Agriculture, and R. W. Thatcher, director of the New York Experiment Station (12, p. 218). William M. Jardine was appointed later (5, p. 123).

The addition of academicians to other departments was not as great as it was in agriculture, but a few very vital positions were filled by people associated with the academic world. In 1921 Harding appointed former President Taft Chief Justice of the Supreme Court. Taft was technically a professor at Yale from 1913 to 1921, but he had numerous other interests. In this regard Pringle stated: "He was away from New Haven as much as he was there" (151, p. 856). There would seem to be little question but that Taft's appointment was based on something other than his academic accomplishments. On the other hand, the appointment of Thomas W. Swan, dean of the Yale Law School, to a judgeship on the Circuit Court could definitely be attributed to his academic accomplishments (132, p. 174).

Coolidge appointed an academician to his cabinet in addition to Jardine. Harlan F. Stone had been a member of a law firm about a year when appointed attorney general, but for a number of years he had been dean of the Columbia Law School (132, p. 220). After Harlan's brief but very successful period as attorney general, Coolidge nominated him to the Supreme Court, and Franklin D. Roosevelt subsequently elevated him to the position of Chief Justice (132, pp. 276, 278). Academicians were also added to lower level positions in the Justice Department as illustrated by the addition, in 1924, of Paul S. Andrews from the law college at Syracuse (29, p. 20).

Two academicians who remained in the State Department after outstanding performances in connection with the peace making were Stanley K. Hornbeck and Arthur N. Young. Young was head of the Economic Adviser's office until 1929. Hornbeck was an adviser to Secretary of State Hughes at the Washington Conferences (1921-22) expert on Far Eastern Affairs in Office of Economic Adviser, and by the 1930's chief of the Division of Far Eastern Affairs (182, pp. 267, 294, 307). Harding named Jacob Gould Schurman, former president of Cornell, minister to China in 1921, and in 1925 Coolidge moved him to Berlin (182, pp. 263, 281).

After his term on the Tariff Commission expired, William S. Culbertson represented the United States in Rumania (1925-28) and in Chile

(1928-33) (29, p. 187). S. H. Cross of Western Reserve served as commercial attache' in Europe in the early twenties before becoming chief of the European Division in the Department of Commerce (29, p. 185). A specialist in Latin American history, Dana G. Munro became a member of the Latin American Division of the State Department Staff in 1921 after earning a doctorate at Pennsylvania and teaching at Georgetown. He was named assistant chief of the Division in 1923 and became its head in 1929. He was also a representative of the United States in Panama, Nicaragua, and Haiti (29, p. 598). From 1923 to 1925 Charles C. Hyde, longtime professor of law at Northwestern University, was solicitor in the Department. Irwin Stewart of the University of Texas began his affiliation with the government as assistant solicitor in 1926 (29, pp. 408, 795).

Academicians came into other areas of government service, and some of those appointed prior to Harding and Coolidge were promoted. George K. Burgess had been in the Bureau of Standards since 1903; in 1913 he was named chief of a division in the Bureau, and in 1923 he became director of the Bureau (23, p. 312). In 1883 Elwood Mead was professor of mathematics at Colorado Agricultural College, and in 1924 Coolidge named him U.S. Commissioner of Reclamation. During the intervening 41 years he had worked with the USDA, served as state engineer in Colorado and Wyoming, and for a number of years was a professor at the University of California (136, p. 528).

The Department of Commerce made greater use of academicians in the twenties than it had prior to the war. Herbert Hoover's policies as

Secretary of Commerce and increased trade resulting from the war were

two of the factors responsible for the increased use of academicians.

Julius Klein was head of the department's Bureau of Foreign and Domestic

Commerce from 1921 to 1929 (98, p. 62). Klein had been on the faculty

at Harvard beginning in 1910, except for a two-year period of service

with the Department of Commerce during World War I (29, p. 455). E.

Dana Durand, in government service since the beginning of the century,

served in the Department of Commerce during the entire decade and became

chief economist for the United States Tariff Commission in 1930 (29, p.

231).

Other academicians were added to the Department of Commerce in the

twenties. Rufus S. Tucker left Harvard to become senior economic ana-

lyst and after two years took a similar position with the Treasury

Department (29, p. 839). The Department also enticed Franklin W. Ryan

from Harvard in 1925 by naming him assistant chief of the Finance Divi-

sion. Personnel from higher education were also found in the Department

of Labor and Treasury.

The commissions and agencies that came into their own prior to the

war provided academicians with a major opportunity for service. However,

the more conservative approach to the regulatory agencies favored by

Harding and Coolidge was revealed by their appointments of fewer academi-

cians to the agencies (91, p. 65). Their attitude toward the function

of these bodies is embodied in the following statement by a biographer

of Coolidge: "Under his and Harding's administrations the character of

the commission's work changed from regulation of business abuses to encouragement of business freedom" (132, p. 285). Academicians were engaged by the commissions as experts, but neither of these Presidents made an initial appointment of an academician to a regulatory commission.

During the twenties the commissions made use of the expertise which academicians possessed. Academicians found that there was a great demand for their services in the United States Tariff Commission. Some of those employed were Percy W. Bidwell of Yale; Dilworth Walker, who had taught at Cornell and Weber College; Abraham W. Fox of City College of New York; Mark A. Smith, who had taught at the University of Kansas prior to the war; and Carlton C. Rice, who had taught in several colleges between 1897 and 1911 and had been in government service since 1911 (29, pp. 65, 278, 686, 772, 859).

A. C. Miller, A democrat initially appointed to the Federal Reserve Board by Wilson, was reappointed by Coolidge (90, p. 130). Alfred P. Dennis was appointed to the Tariff Commission in 1925 after serving with Hoover in the Department of Commerce. Dennis received a Ph. D. degree at Princeton, taught at Wesleyan and Smith College, and wrote about trade and industry prior to joining the Commission (90, pp. 116, 131). A highly trained agricultural economist, Edgar B. Brossard, became a member of the Tariff Commission in 1925. Prior to his appointment, he had earned a Ph. D. degree at the University of Minnesota and had taught at Utah Agricultural College (90, p. 116). In 1923 he was preparing to take a leave to do research at Harvard when a request came to the president of Utah Agricultural College for an expert on sugar beet cost. Brossard decided he could do research in Washington as well as at Harvard.

Neither the money nor the position attracted him but the challenge of the work was enough to cause him to change his plans. After two years as an economist with the Commission he was given a commissionship (90, pp. 36, 62).

In 1927 Congress passed the White-Dill Radio Bill, creating a Federal Radio Commission of five members appointed by the President with the approval of the Senate (49, p. 302). The Commission was replaced in 1934, but of the men appointed between 1927 and 1934 only one could be classified as an academician (90). Henry A. Bellows received a doctorate from Harvard, taught rhetoric at the University of Wisconsin, and was a member of the English faculty at the University of Minnesota (90, p. 120; 29, p. 987). He then went into the newspaper business and was manager of the Gold Medal Radio Corporation prior to his appointment to the Commission (90, p. 120). Academicians were found serving the Federal Reserve Board, the Children's Bureau, and other agencies that needed technical assistance. Congressional committees continued to invite scholars to testify before them and continued the practice of engaging academicians to provide technical advice and assistance.

Before discussing the developments of the Hoover administration, the academicians actively involved in politics will be discussed briefly. As stated earlier, academicians generally tended to avoid politics in the twenties, but there were exceptions. Simeon D. Fess, who served in the United States House of Representatives from 1912 to 1922, was elected to the Senate in 1922 and re-elected in 1928 (67, p. 340). A fellow Ohio academician, Frank Bartlett Willis, was returned to Congress in 1921.

After serving in the House of Representatives, he was elected governor of Ohio; he later made two unsuccessful attempts to regain the governorship. By 1920 he was far from unknown in the national Republican Party, as is shown by his being asked to place Harding's name before the national convention (207, p. 445). Hiram Bingham, a historian at Yale, made his maiden voyage in national politics in this period. In the election of 1924, the voters in Connecticut selected Bingham to represent them in the United States Senate and also elected him governor of the state. He chose the Senate even though he was elected to complete an unexpired term, but he was successful in his bid for a full term in 1926 (153, p. 429). It should also be remembered that Henry Cabot Lodge's service in the Senate continued into the early twenties (77). An interesting sidelight is that all four were members of the Republican Party. Still in the political realm, Nicholas Murray Butler, referred to by one writer as the Republican party's "intellectual-in-chief," played an active part in the national conventions held during the decade (132, pp. 245, 293). William E. Dodd was interested in the direction that the Democratic Party took in the twenties, but he had very little influence on party policies, and of the election of 1928 he said: "There is no place this year for men who knew and believed in Woodrow Wilson " (50, p. 144).

The movements for social, political, and other reforms diminished in the twenties, but the feeling remained alive partly through the efforts of academicians. John R. Commons and Felix Frankfurter were among the more active of this group (91, p. 86). This study does not deal directly with the relationship between reform and public service, but through

the early years of the nineteen hundreds there was a connection between
the two, and the relationship was revived in the thirties.

Herbert Hoover's Administration

Herbert Hoover had more in common with the academic world than his
two immediate predecessors in the White House. Although he never earned
an advanced degree, he became known to the academic world through his
writings, through his working with academicians (especially in the Food
Administration), and also through relief efforts. Hoover also had
close contact with the academic community during the period in which
he was Secretary of Commerce and through his association with his alma
mater, Stanford University. When he assumed the Presidency, he appointed a leading academician, Ray Lyman Wilbur, Secretary of Interior. Wilbur graduated from Stanford a year after Hoover and continued his college
work by earning a M.D. degree. He also taught in the fields of physiology and medicine before becoming president of Stanford (85, p. 53). In
addition to serving in the cabinet, Wilbur was in the inner circle of
Hoover's advisers. The leading role which he played in the administration is shown by his long association with Hoover and by his background
and personal characteristics which President Hoover cited when discussing
the appointment:

> He was President of Stanford University, and his long back-
> ground in public phases of the medical profession prior to
> his university presidency gave him a fine insight into social
> and educational forces so much needed by the Interior Depart-
> ment at that period. He was a great outdoor man and knew
> the West and its resources above most men (98, p. 220).

Wilbur was alone in the official cabinet as far as academicians were concerned; however, Harlan F. Stone, the academician earlier appointed to the Supreme Court, became an intimate of Hoover's and was a member of an inner circle referred to as Hoover's "Medicine Ball Cabinet" (170, p. 462).

On the large scene of national problems, Hoover appointed two groups to study various aspects of American life, and academicians were associated with both groups. The eleven-member National Committee on Law Observance and Enforcement, more commonly known as the Wickersham Commission, was appointed in May, 1929, to investigate and recommend action related to crime and prohibition. Dean Roscoe Pound of the Harvard Law School and President Ada Comstock of Radcliffe College were members of the Commission (98, p. 277). The Commission also utilized the services of academicians in collecting the information and in writing the report. Serving in such a capacity were Harold A. Phelps, professor of sociology at the University of Pittsburgh; Jesse F. Steiner of the University of Washington; and Paul S. Taylor, professor of economics at the University of California (29, pp. 651, 791, 817).

Hoover also appointed a committee to study social conditions in the nation; this was known as the Committee on Recent Social Trends in the United States. Two of the seven directing members were academicians--Wesley C. Mitchell and Charles E. Merriam (98, p. 312). Mitchell was given the added honor of being named chairman. He received a Ph. D. degree from Chicago in 1896 and taught several years at the nation's leading universities in addition to working with the government and with several foundations (29, p. 578). The publication in

1913 of his epoch-making statistical study on economic trends in the United States entitled Business Cycles established him as a pioneer in the field of research on the economic process (46, p. 51).

Charles E. Merriam's involvement in government affairs dated from the turn of the century, but serving on the Committee on Recent Social Trends was his first involvement at the national level except during World War I. While earning a doctorate at Columbia University he studied the Tammany Hall operation and took part in a mayoralty campaign, followed by a year's study in Berlin as the student of a Dr. Preuss, who was also a member of the Berlin City Council (203, p. 7). Merriam then joined the faculty at the University of Chicago and took an active part in city politics. He was elected to the Chicago City Council, and in 1911 was an unsuccessful candidate for mayor of Chicago (203, p. 6). Merriam was offered several important posts in Washington, such as membership on President Taft's Commission on Economy and Efficiency and a twelve-year term on a board during Wilson's administration. He declined all offers except the opportunity to be of service to the nation during World War I (203, pp. 9, 14). His acceptance of the vice-chairmanship of Hoover's Committee on Recent Social Trends brought an important member of the academic community into government service and one who was familiar with politics from the standpoints of theory and practice.

The Committee made extensive use of academicians in research on the project and in compiling the lengthy report. William F. Ogburn, who had been at the University of Chicago since 1927, was director of research (29, p. 622). Gutav Peck, who had earned a Ph. D. degree in 1927, and

P. K. Whelpton, a former professor at Texas Agricultural and Mechanical College, were on Ogburn's staff (29, pp. 643, 886). Much of the investigation was done by S. Colum Gilfillan, a former professor at Grinnell College; Malcome M. Willey, a professor and administrator at the University of Minnesota; and T. J. Woofter, professor at the University of North Carolina (29, pp. 304, 897, 915). Others closely associated with the committee were Ralph G. Hurlin of the Russell Sage Foundation, J.H. Korb of Wisconsin, Jesse F. Steiner of the University of Wisconsin, and Irene B. Taeuber of Mt. Holyoke College (29, pp. 406, 461, 791, 812).

The USDA continued its use of academicians, and many of those mentioned in the section on Harding and Coolidge remained in the Department. The need for economists persisted especially in the Bureau of Agricultural Economics. Fred L. Garlock left a teaching position at Iowa State College to become a senior economist in the Bureau, and W. H. Rowe joined the Bureau after teaching at Kansas State Agricultural College and the University of Akron (29, pp. 393, 711). J. M. Tinley came to the USDA as an inspector but was promoted to an economist after completing requirements for a Ph. D. degree at Minnesota in 1928, and E. J. Working left a teaching position at Minnesota to take a position as economist with the Bureau (29, pp. 830, 916).

Lynn R. Edminister received a Ph. D. degree in 1930 and commenced government service in the USDA the same year (29, p. 238). After a brief teaching career, Mrs. Faith M. Williams joined the Bureau of Home Economics (29, p. 989). In 1931 the Forest Service added an academician who had been teaching at North Carolina since 1926--Paul W. Wager (29, p. 857).

In the light of the developments in the thirties, one of the most significant accomplishments of the USDA during Hoover's administration was the passage of an act in 1929 creating the Federal Farm Board. The act provided for an eight-member board appointed by the President to carry out the provisions of the act. Charles S. Wilson, former professor of agriculture at Cornell, was the only academician on the board (98, p. 255), but others were brought to Washington to assist the board in its work. In 1931 the board brought Milburn L. Wilson to Washington. Wilson had been active in extension work in South Dakota, Iowa, and Montana from 1906 to 1924, and was on the faculty at Montana State College when he joined the Department (5, pp. 136, 451). Wilson joined Mordecai Ezekiel in working on numerous plans generally referred to as domestic allotment plans. The foundation work for many of the New Deal agricultural programs was laid during this period, and academicians were the principal planners.

Harry N. Owen, a journalist, is credited with presenting the first domestic allotment plan for farm relief, but the plan was actually a synthesis of ideas originated by others (5, p. 135). William J. Spillman of the USDA outlined the idea in a book published in 1927 entitled Balancing the Farm Output and the plan provided for farm allotments, processing taxes, and benefit payments (5, p. 135; 53, p. 4). John D. Black of Harvard suggested a similar program in his book, Agricultural Reform in the United States (1929), and testified on the topic before Congressional committees (12, pp. 239, 267). George F. Warren of Cornell influenced thought and later policy in the fields of price ratios

and monetary action in conjunction with price levels (53, p. 5). The
domestic allotment plan was modified and publicized by Beardsley Ruml,
an academician with the Laura Spelman Rockefeller Memorial Foundation
(5, p. 136). Wilson had contributed to and studied domestic allotment
while a faculty member at Montana State, but after joining the USDA he
was in a better position to get more support for the plan (5, p. 136;
50, p. 5). The proposals reached fruition during the New Deal, with
Wilson and other academicians planning and administering the programs.
The Grange also developed a proposal in the twenties, based largely on
the work of Charles L. Stewart, a professor at the University of Illinois, which came to be known as the Export Debenture Plan (12, p. 226).

Some interesting events took place in the State Department involv-
ing the services of academicians during Hoover's presidency. James
Grafton Rogers, dean of the law school at the University of Colorado,
was named assistant Secretary of State in 1931. He had had no experience in governmental or international matters, but Secretary of State
Stimson used him as a liaison officer with the press. Roger's unusual
success in this role could probably be attributed to his experience as
a newspaperman (5, p. 294). His appointment was wholly political in
character, and his services were terminated with the new administration
in 1933 (5, p. 311).

Hoover replaced Jardine as Secretary of Agriculture but then
appointed him minister to Egypt (205, p. 586). It appeared to many
that this appointment was also based primarily on politics. Two other
academicians occupied important positions in the State Department in

this period. Herbert Feis entered the department in 1931 as Economic Adviser (182, p. 307). Feis had received a Ph. D. degree at Harvard in 1921 and had taught at Kansas and the University of Cincinnati in addition to making his expertise available to municipal, state, and international groups (29, p. 260). Tyler Dennett, a historian of high reputation, had been chief of the Division of Publications since 1924. In 1929 his designation was changed to Historical Adviser, a position he held until 1931 (182, p. 296). The Congress in 1925 and again in 1929 authroized the publication of the official papers of the Territories of the United States, and the work was initiated in 1931 under the direction of Clarence E. Carter (182, p. 296). Carter had a Ph. D. degree from the University of Illinois and had taught history at Illinois College, at Miami of Ohio, and at the University of Texas (29, p. 134). Carter was assisted in the work by Fred W. Shipman, who had experience as a college professor and as a librarian (29, p. 754).

The Department of Commerce added a number of academicians to those brought in earlier while Hoover was Secretary of Commerce. Julius Klein, Hoover's friend and former associate in the Department, was promoted from director of the Bureau for Foreign and Domestic Commerce to assistant secretary of Commerce (114, p. 23). Dana E. Durand, who had moved through many government agencies since 1900, served as statistical adviser to the secretary in 1929 and 1930 (29, p. 231). Rowland Burnston held a variety of positions in higher education, industry, and state government before his short stay in the Department of Commerce as an economist (29, p. 117). By contrast in years of service, John R.

Riggleman began working for the Department in 1929 as an economist and remained in government work until the post-World War II era (29, p. 692).

The Census Bureau, an agency within the Department of Commerce, had made extensive use of academicians from the late nineteenth century. During this period Theodore N. Beckman, a professor of economics at Ohio State, served as a consultant in charge of wholesale distribution (29, p. 53). N. H. Engle left a teaching position at the University of Michigan to accept a position in the Census Bureau in 1930, and in 1933 he was transferred to the Bureau of Foreign and Domestic Commerce (29, p. 248). The Census Bureau added Charles E. Persons from Harvard as an expert on the economics of unemployment in 1929 (29, p. 647). In 1930 Warren S. Thompson, director of Scripps Foundation for Research in Population Problems, served as a special adviser to the Bureau (29, p. 826).

Hoover used academicians sparingly in filling positions on the regulatory commissions. John L. Coulter served as a commissioner on the United States Tariff Commission from 1930 to 1934. After receiving a Ph. D. degree at the University of Wisconsin, he taught in three western state universities and did special work for the Census Bureau. He then became dean of West Virginia Agricultural College, and in 1921 he became president of North Dakota Agricultural and Mining College (90, p. 116). He resigned in 1929 to become chief economist and Chairman of the Board of Advisers on the Tariff Commission (90, p. 37). When he was named commissioner in 1930, E. Dana Durand became the Commission's chief economist (29, p. 231). Hoover appointed Thomas W. Page to a new term on the Tariff Commission in 1930. He had resigned as a commissioner in 1923 but accepted another term after the Commission was reorganized in 1930 (90, p. 62)

Charles D. Mahaffie was elevated to the Interstate Commerce Commission in 1930 following a number of years in government service. He began government work in the Department of Interior prior to World War I and moved to the I.C.C. in 1922. After eight years in the Bureau of Finance he was named a member of the Commission (90, pp. 47, 64). One authority on the commissions characterized his appointment as " the clearest case of an intelligent college graduate who finally secured a commissionship through ability and training" (90, p. 64).

In 1930 Congress reorganized the Federal Power Commission through the Water Power Act, which provided for a commission of five members appointed by the President with the approval of the Senate (49, pp. 286-87). George O. Smith was the only academician on the original commission, but he had the added honor of being selected chairman. Since the early 1900's he had been director of the Geological Survey (90, p. 51).

Hoover also appointed a man with an academic background to the Supreme Court. Owen Josephus Roberts was a lawyer first, but in addition to practicing law from 1898 to 1918 he was a member of the law faculty at the University of Pennsylvania. In the mid-twenties, President Coolidge appointed Roberts special prosecutor in the Elk Hills and Teapot Dome oil lease frauds. Hoover then appointed him to the Court in 1930 (158, p. 88). Roberts' selection brought the number of academicians nominated and appointed to the Court in the period from 1921 to

1933 to three. This is another indication that the decade of the twenties was not as barren of academicians as is sometimes indicated. The period served as a springboard for the New Deal because ideas were germinating and academicians were becoming available for the opportunities that opened up to them when Franklin D. Roosevelt moved into the White House.

CHAPTER V

ACADEMICIANS AND THE FIRST YEARS OF THE NEW DEAL

Use of Academicians

Various interest groups have traditionally been associated with periods in the history of the United States, such as the businessman in the post-Civil War era. Similar to this influence was the influence of academicians in the first years of the New Deal. This chapter deals with the factors that contributed to the greater involvment of academicians in governmental activities and with many of the leading academic personalities of the New Deal.

Franklin D. Roosevelt's education and most of his activities prior to becoming governor of New York indicated no special affinity for or attraction to academicians. The surprise expressed by the American people toward his use of academicians may have been based partly on his previous actions. However, while serving as governor of New York and while campaigning for the presidency in 1932, he relied heavily on them. In New York state he used academicians for developing a penal reform program and appointed Walter N. Thayer, a psychiatrist and penologist, State Commissioner of Correction (11, p. 33). He also appointed a group which included academicians to develop a twenty-year public health plan for New York state (120, p. 21).

As governor he habitually consulted with Robert M. Haig, William I. Myers, Frank A. Pearson, James C. Bonbright, Raymond Moley, and other academicians (140, p. 5). In January of 1931 Roosevelt met with six governors and the representative of another at a conference which studied the government's responsibility in relief and unemployment. Academicians speaking before the group were Paul H. Douglas, professor at the University of Chicago; Leo Wolman of the Amalgamated Clothing Workers of America; William Leiserson of Antioch College; and Joseph P. Chamberlain of Columbia University (11, p. 185). Rexford G. Tugwell, a member of the "brain trust," credited Roosevelt with using commissions freely and skillfully while governor of New York (187, p. 208). One of the factors that might have foreshadowed Roosevelt's intentions concerning the use of academicians was his practice in New York. Yet, as Ernest K. Lindley stated after reviewing Roosevelt's activities as governor: "No one had heard of 'brains trust'" (120, p. 21).

Another barometer of his attitude toward academicians was the use he made of academicians during the campaign of 1932. In making preparations for the campaign, Roosevelt brought together a group of expert advisers that became known as the "brains trust." There has been some question about the spelling of the designation and about its origin. Raymond Moley credited Jimmy Kieran of the New York Times with first using the term (140, p. 9), while Joseph Alsop and Robert Kintner said that Roosevelt's confidant, Louis M. Howe, first used the term (3, p.3). Regardless of who originated the term and how it was spelled, the group contributed much to the campaign. Originally it was devoted to drafting speeches, but during the campaign and following the election the group evolved into a continuing seminar on emergency measures related to the depression (75, p. 207). The original brain trust included Samuel I. Rosenman and the academicians from Columbia University: Raymond Moley, Rexford G. Tugwell, and Adolf A. Berle (75, p. 207). Until Roosevelt's inauguration the group remained more or less cohesive but as will be shown, it began to break up following the inauguration. Others were brought in for consultation and for writing speeches or position papers on particular issues, so that in the popular mind many of the experts began to be considered members of the brain trust (120, p. 297).

Considering Roosevelt's association with academicians prior to his becoming President, it does not seem surprising that he used the number he did in the federal government. From a contemporary viewpoint, it might appear strange that Americans would consider Roosevelt's actions radical. In this connection, there were at least two conditions that were different concerning the academicians in the New Deal as compared with those in the other periods in this study. First, the number involved was greater than even the other peak period--World War I. Second, the academicians were given a greater role in policymaking and in administration of programs. In this regard, it is ironical that, except for Harding, every President since 1913 had had at least one academician in his cabinet; yet the administration that was most noted for its association with the academic world had none. It is also important to note that academicians did not influence policymaking during the New Deal as much as the public may have thought. Newspapers and magazine tended to focus on the academician in government in the early phase of the New Deal, causing undue attention to this new creature in government. Claude C. Bowman concluded from his analysis that it was "popularly assumed that college professors never participated in political affairs before 1933" (16, p. 158). He noted that this was not the case, for they had long associations with governmental activities, although they never had been so prominent nor excited so much comment (16, p. 158).

There is some question concerning the origin of the decision by Roosevelt to lean heavily on academicians. An early book-length account of the personnel of the New Deal credits Samuel I. Rosenman with suggesting the use of professors. According to this account, during a discussion of the Hoover debacle by Roosevelt and Rosenman the latter suggested going to the universities for a change and giving the job of national problems to professional experts (3, p. 20). Rosenman indicated in his work on the Roosevelt years that this was generally how the idea emerged (164, p. 57). On the other hand, Moley raised a pertinent question concerning the manner in which the decision was reached. He did not doubt that such a conversation took place, but he had trouble believing that a man who had been closely associated with Roosevelt for two years would make such a suggestion to a former governor who had habitually consulted with academicians (140, p. 5). As Moley concluded it seems a logical extension of Roosevelt's practices as governor and a continuation of the use of the type of personnel heavily relied on during the campaign. Regardless of the reasons for the decision, academicians were brought into the Roosevelt administration, and the number involved was significant.

The conditions that prompted the unprecedented influx of academicians into Washington were not greatly unlike the conditions in 1917. As one author stated, "There was the overwhelming pressure for emergency measures that mark wartime action" (61, p. 209). Another factor that influenced Roosevelt's decision to bring academic people into public life was the prevailing attitude toward the businessmen, industrialists, and political leaders who had been dominant in the government in the twenties (112, p. 459). There was a reaction against the businessman and the financier as a result of the depression, and the academicians were in a favorable position to fill the void (83, p. 108). Leo Gurko took the position that intellectuals have been called on only in times of distress when conventional solutions have failed. In his opinion this made the important role of the academician during the New Deal possible:

> When the depression hit bottom in 1933, familiar attitudes were so shaken from their moorings that it was possible for Franklin D. Roosevelt...to import to Washington a whole corps of professors of law, economics, and political science ...without anyone raising a cry of protest--at least not during the early months (83, p. 103).

Like men of any age and profession, the academic people of the New Deal represented many shades of thought and a number of specialties, but there was something unique about many of the brain trusters: they were enthusiastic about the American way of life but at the same time critical of its course of development. The overriding feature of the early years of the Roosevelt administration was free competition in ideas and frank criticism (120, p. 315). This may be one of the explanations for the mortality rate among the members of the Roosevelt administration and especially among the academicians. There were other characteristics of the academicians that commended them to a President in the position of Roosevelt. Because of their trained minds and academic backgrounds they were equipped to handle large and novel problems without much of the usual hankering for political success or financial reward (3, p.10). The following statement indicates where many of the academicians placed their priorities:

> They are, in fact, reasonably disinterested men, chiefly desirous of seeing their ideas become realities, and satisfied with that as their price. Therefore, the President has been able to rely on them for the reasonably honest spending of the New Deal's billions and for the reasonably efficient exercise of the New Deal's immense and complex powers (3, p. 10).

It has also been suggested that Roosevelt turned to the colleges and universities because he needed neutrals--someone who didn't smell of Wall Street but by the same token would not too greatly scare the wealthy. In addition, he needed people who had the brains, competence, and willingness to implement the policies agreed upon (139, p. 743). There is much evidence to indicate that academicians were far from neutral, unless neutral is considered as a point halfway between Huey Long and Wall Street (139, p. 742). Nevertheless, Moley and Berle are good examples of disinterested professors. Moley thought Roosevelt would win in 1932, but he indicated that his decision to aid in the campaign was based on a desire to know what went on at the heart of politics and not because he had any political ambitions (140, p. 3). Moley viewed

serving with Roosevelt in New York in a similar way. In Moley's words,

it was "an opportunity to satisfy my desire for a wider experience in

politics and, at the same time, to help, in a small way, in the realiza-

tion of old and time-tested concepts of political evolution" (140, p.5).

Berle's lack of interest in personal advancement in politics is best

revealed by his lack of interest in Roosevelt as a candidate in the pre-

convention days; yet upon request he submitted an excellent memorandum

on federal finances (121, p. 259).

If men like Moley and Berle and many other New Dealers had a sel-

fish interest in the New Deal, it was in getting a system established

that they thought would be best for the nation and not an interest in

financial and political rewards. The change in Berle's attitude toward

Roosevelt probably came about because he realized that Roosevelt was

the type of man in public life for whom he had been searching (121,

p. 259). Tugwell's attitude toward service is representative of a

large number of academicians. He thought that economists should plot

the course of the modern world, and that it was the duty of politicians

like Roosevelt to put their ideas into effect (121, p. 263).

Another factor which was influential in bringing academicians into

government was the nature of new ventures sponsored by the New Deal.

Among these were the Security and Exchange Commission, Social Security,

Agricultural Adjustment, Regional Planning (TVA), and the National Labor

Relations Board (3, p. 189). Other administrations had experienced new

ventures, such as the Federal Trade Commission and the Federal Reserve

Board, but none could compare with the first years of the Roosevelt administration with regard to speed, intensity, and number. The new ventures of the thirties also compounded the trend toward complexity in government that had been under way for years in the country. Trained people were required; thus, nothing now seemed more absurd than William J. Bryan's hoary dictum: "Any man with real goodness of heart can write a good currency law" (3, p. 191). The complexity of government prompted the observation that hacks and amateurs in government were insufficient, and in the words of Joseph Alsop and Robert Kintner: "It is now necessary to have men in every department and agency capable of taking the economic data, reading their meaning, and coordinating government policy in terms of that meaning. Only thoroughgoing experts can do the work" (3, p. 193). The increase in the technical nature of government, coupled with the lack of Democrats with government experience (since the Republicans had been in power since 1920), narrowed Roosevelt's choices for filling government posts.

Before taking up some of the personalities of the New Deal, it might be useful to consider again the position of higher education on public service. In Chapter II it was pointed out that for years colleges and universities strongly endorsed the idea of public service. Chronologically, the discussion ended with the early twentieth century, so the attempt at this point is to show briefly that this position continued into the thirties. Even though in Chapter II the discussion of the public service attitude in higher education terminated with the early years of the twentieth century, public services was still a

dominant theme by the thirties. Addresses delivered between 1921 and
1933 by Lotus D. Coffman, President of the University of Minnesota, indicated that he viewed public service as one of the basic functions of
a university. On one occasion Coffman declared: "Another of the general functions of the university, quite as important as the development
of a generous, intelligent, and discriminating spirit of cosmopolitan-
ism, is that of service to the community or state in which the university is located" (34, p. 21). Coffman did not limit the service to
state and local governments but included service to the national government.

Public service was given in 1936 as one argument for a national
university: "The chief justification for a national university arises
out of the fact that our national problems are becoming more numerous
and more complex and more dependent upon scientific and technological
knowledge" (200, p. viii). Walter Lippmann also thought that academicians were concerned about their responsibility to society. In a 1932
Atlantic Monthly article, he said, "In addition to the anxieties which
he shares with all other men in days like these, there is a special
uneasiness which perturbs the scholar. He feels that he ought to be
doing something about the world's troubles, or at least to be saying
something about them" (126, p. 148). Roosevelt recognized that higher
education had developed a strong utilitarian approach and that academicians were anxious to serve the government (113, p. 471).

Before the individuals are discussed, some general observations
should be made about the nature of their service and public reaction

to it. Even though Roosevelt did use academicians extensively, he did
not turn the government over to them nor did he rely on them to the extent that businessmen and bankers were forgotten about. These seem to
be two of the most erroneous views held by people at the time the New
Deal was developing. One contemporary magazine writer complimented
Roosevelt for bringing academicians to Washington and suggested that
the public considered this as evidence that he intended to run the
government more intelligently than any of his predecessors (134, p.340).
But the same person thought FDR permitted the brain trust too much lati-
tude in experimenting during such perilous times (134, p. 345).

Another magazine declared in an editorial that the public objected
to the power and responsibility given to academic people since they
were determined to put untested theories into practice during a time of
crisis (18, p. 22). The use of academicians was supported by other writers using a number of justifications. Frank R. Kent of the Baltimore
Sun viewed the collaboration of the practical politician and the students of economics and public questions as an ideal combination (129,
p. 9). Academicians also had the advantage over members of Congress
and heads of executive departments in that they had more time to study
questions and could do so with a greater degree of detachment from
prejudice and special interest (154, p. 711). Therefore, it is apparent that feeling was divided concerning the academician, with a major
concern being the undue influence that theoriticians might wield. The
view that a clique of academicians operated the government under Roosevelt is incorrect (17, p. 20). The financiers and businessmen did not

continue to have the inside track that they had in the twenties, but their presence was still realized in Washington (169, pp. 87-176). The influence of businessmen is apparent when one considers the appointments to the new agencies. For example, Joseph P. Kennedy, the epitome of American entrepreneurs, was appointed chairman of the Securities and Exchange Commission (169, p. 468). In summary, academicians exerted a greater influence on the national government during the New Deal than they ever had, but they certainly did not control the country.

Brain Trusters

A discussion of the academicians in the New Deal is difficult since they were so numerous, and as compared with the World War I era the number who held prominent positions was much greater. Therefore, only those appointed to or promoted to significant positions are included in the text of this chapter, and other academicians associated with the New Deal are listed in the appendix. This is not necessarily intended as a delineation between levels of positions. In some cases, considerations other than position on the organization chart dictated the placing of a name in the body of the chapter.

Rather than beginning with academicians in the departments and agencies as has been done in the preceding chapters, this chapter will deal first with a few of the academicians who had an overall influence on the administration. Raymond Moley probably deserves first consideration in this regard since he helped organize the original brain trust and since he played a very substantial role in the first few months of

the new administration. Moley was born in Ohio and received his first
two degrees from colleges in Ohio, followed by a doctorate from Columbia (120, p. 298). By the time he emerged as a national figure he had
gained a wide range of experiences in education and in government. Most
of his government experience resulted from serving as adviser and consultant to governors and commissions, but at 21 he was elected mayor
of Berea, Ohio (140, p. 3). Later he was director of americanization
activities under Governor James M. Cox in Ohio; a consultant for crime
surveys in Illinois, Pennsylvania, and Virginia; and research director
of the New York State Crime Commission in 1926 and 1927 (75, p. 215;
119, p. 3). In 1931 he became research director of the New York Crime
Commission. This led to his close association with Roosevelt and the
1932 request to team with Basil O'Connor and Samuel I. Rosenman in re-
cruiting the brain trust (75, pp. 215-16).

Moley's invitations to assist the various states came about as a
result of his academic achievements. After teaching at Western Reserve, he became a member of the faculty at Columbia University, where
he developed a substantial reputation in government and public law (75,
p. 215). Moley apparently had little interest in a position in the
new administration (169, p. 181), but Roosevelt persuaded him to accept
the post of Assistant Secretary of State. Moley was specifically responsible for economic affairs and was an intimate adviser to Roosevelt
(182, pp. 309-11). The arrangement was cumbersome for all concerned,
and Moley was soon out of the government but continued to consult with
Roosevelt for some time. Jim Farley, who was one of the master

politicians of the administration, considered Moley one of the ablest men serving under Roosevelt in the early days. Farley's assessment of Moley is expressed in the following statement: "He had a brilliant, analytical mind and a gift for marshalling ideas on paper. Unfortunately for him, he lacked schooling in the rough and tumble academy of practical politics" (65, p. 41). The case of Moley and the London Economic Conference also reveals a fundamental point concerning the relative strengths of academicians and politicians. When Moley and Secretary of State Cordell Hull disagreed on the vital monetary issue, Moley was the one who had to go. At this point, no professor could have been as valuable to Roosevelt as a loyal Democrat (139, p. 740).

Another member of the original brain trust was Adolf A. Berle, Jr., a lecturer on corporation law at Columbia and a practicing attorney (17, p. 21). When only nineteen Berle had a Master's degree from Harvard, and at twenty-five he was an economic adviser to the American delegation at Versailles resigning in protest over the treaty (17, p. 21). In the 1920's he taught and practiced law and with Gardiner C. Means published in 1932 The Modern Corporation and Private Property; they set forth the idea that the rise of the modern corporation had revolutionized the economy, which required a revolutionizing in the ways of thinking about public policy (168, p. 190). Berle's background and ideas on government policy made him attractive to the organizers of the brain trust. After making significant contributions to the campaign, he was offered a full-time job in Washington. Even though he turned it down, he averaged approximately half of every week during the first months of the New Deal

as a special adviser to the Reconstruction Finance Corporation, especially on banking and railroad legislation (169, p. 182). Berle's influence eventually permeated many aspects of the government, and in
1938 he became Assistant Secretary of State (182, p. 332).

Moley and Berle were joined in the campaign by a Columbia colleague,
Rexford G. Tugwell. Tugwell earned three degrees, including a Ph.D. at
the University of Pennsylvania (5, p. 450). As a student at Pennsylvania he studied with Simon Patton and Scott Nearing at the Wharton
School, where he picked up the idea of national planning (168, p. 193).
Schlesinger said that Tugwell added to this Thorstein Veblen's concept
that the domination of industry by business condemned man to an age of
scarcity and John Dewey's belief that reason was the instrument with
which to shape the future. To these Tugwell added the scientific management views of Frederick W. Taylor and came up with the techniques by
which society might achieve the ends proposed by those who had most influenced him (168, p. 194).

Tugwell taught economics at the Universities of Pennsylvania and
Washington before moving to Columbia (5, p. 450). He was active during
the campaign of 1932 and, like Moley, appeared to be reluctant to accept
a job in the administration. He agreed to become Assistant Secretary of
Agriculture because he felt the department needed drastic reorganization
and he could do Secretary Wallace's surgery for him (168, p. 473). Since
Tugwell supported Wallace for the cabinet position in Agriculture, it is
not surprising that he himself got the second spot (5, p. 247).

Moley, Berle, and Tugwell had at least two things in common that are noteworthy in this study. They agreed that the government needed to take a more positive role in the economic life of the nation which influenced New Deal policy (75, p. 210), and they all taught at Columbia, which meant that other professors from that school would be brought into government service. However, in the box scores Columbia soon lost to Harvard, thanks to the active interest of Felix Frankfurter. In the final analysis Frankfurter's influence on the administration was as great as or greater than that of any of the three from Columbia. Frankfurter came to the United States from Vienna when twelve years old. After graduating from the College of City of New York and Harvard Law School, he worked with Henry L. Stimson when Stimson was United States Attorney in New York (168, p. 418). In 1914 he became a professor at Harvard Law School and already had eight years of experience in public service (66, p. 88). Like many other academicians, he aided in the war effort. During the war years Frankfurter served in the War Department, as assistant to the Secretary of Labor, and chairman of the War Labor Policies Board (66, p. 88).

Frankfurter had frequent contacts with Roosevelt following their initial meeting in the early twentieth century. They were in Washington together during part of Wilson's administration (168, pp. 418-19), and Roosevelt frequently sought his advice while he was governor of New York (120, p. 29). When Roosevelt was elected President, he proposed that Frankfurter become Solicitor General. Frankfurter refused on the grounds that he could be more help outside government service (170, p. 225). He

served the administration and often worked more or less independently
and without much publicity (120, p. 29). One example of this type of
contribution was in connection with the securities bill. As the original draft of it was unsatisfactory to some, Moley requested Frankfurter to revise it. His proposal was revised in turn by Congress but
served as the basis for the new law (120, p. 107).

Frankfurter's most significant indirect contribution was in recom-
mending individuals for positions in government. It was in this way
that Harvard got the jump on Columbia in the number in government service. Berle pointed out that Columbia might have been the early intellectual home of the New Deal, but that its later home was plainly the
Harvard Law School (170, p. 393). As early as the fall of 1933 one
magazine writer recognized the sagacious Frankfurter as the force behind
the brain trust, advising, counseling, but staying out of the spotlight
(15, p. 7). Schlesinger observed that he had "a resourceful approach
to questions of public policy and a passion for raising the standards
of public service" (168, p. 419). Frankfurter proved to be very valuable
to Roosevelt in working outside the administration as an adviser and as
an "employment agency," but Roosevelt eventually appointed him to the
Supreme Court.

There is justification for including others in a discussion of
academicians who had an overall influence on policy, but they will be
included under a department or agency with which they were associated.
As the new administration began its work, the original brain trust grad-
ually lost its identity. Instead, there were various subsidiary brain

trusts and academicians scattered throughout the administration doing their own job (120, p. 298). The remainder of this chapter deals with some of these academicians.

Department of Agriculture

As was generally true throughout the twentieth century, the USDA was in the forefront of government groups using the services of academicians. The new secretary was not an academician, but Tugwell was appointed to the number two position in the Department. Tugwell served as Assistant Secretary until June, 1934, when he was elevated to the newly created post of Under Secretary, a position he held until December 31, 1936 (5, pp. 452-53). The significance of Tugwell's appointment is emphasized in the following statement:

> Selection of a professor of economics from east of the
> Alleghenies without land-grant college connections, who
> had a reputation for brilliant and unorthodox ideas,
> symbolized change in the Department of Agriculture that
> was to plunge it into the swift moving current of con-
> troversial economic and social reforms (5, p. 247).

The new programs, like the agricultural adjustment acts, created a great need for men like Tugwell with training and imagination. Milburn L. Wilson, who came into the Department in the last years of the Hoover administration, also possessed these characteristics. His experiences in the field of agriculture prior to 1933 had been varied. Following his years as a student at Ames, Iowa, he was a homesteader in Montana, a professor of agriculture, a division head in the USDA, and a collaborator on the domestic allotment plan just before the crash in 1929 (169,

p. 36). Wilson discussed agricultural questions with Roosevelt in 1932, and according to one account, after discussing the allotment, Roosevelt suddenly responded, "Have you been telling me your plan, or have I been telling you mine" (11, p. 93). Under the new administration, he was named head of the Wheat Section in the Division of Production provided for by the Agricultural Adjustment Act (5, p. 147). In the late summer of 1933 Wilson helped organize and headed the Division of Subsistence Homesteads created in the Department of Interior and funded under the National Industrial Recovery Act (5, p. 208). When Tugwell was named under secretary, Wilson replaced him as assistant secretary. When Tugwell resigned in 1936, Wilson was named under secretary (5, p.451). It is readily apparent that Wilson's responsibilities in the Department were extensive and that he was able to influence policy and programs.

L. C. Gray joined the Department in the post-World War I period and in the thirties directed the first nationwide program of land retirement in the Agricultural Adjustment Administration (156, p. 218). As a result of the emphasis of the New Deal farm programs on economics, Secretary Wallace created the position of economic adviser to the secretary and selected Mordecai Ezekiel for the new position (5, p. 247). He had been in the Department for a decade and had aided in the work on the domestic allotment plan. Ezekiel's role was greatly enlarged under the new administration; initially he served as a major adviser in selecting personnel and in drafting new legislation (5, p. 247; 155, p. 497). In economic affairs he was joined by Louis Bean, a master statistician in the Department and by Gardner Means, an economist who had close ties with Berle and Tugwell (168, pp. 190-91; 169, p. 51). Bean's experience in economic forecasting was helpful in making decisions on the application of adjustment programs to commodities and to problems. Bean was also economic adviser to the Agricultural Adjustment Administration (5, p. 247). Mean's specialty was the modern corporation; therefore, his major responsibility was to advise on programs and activities outside the Department that might infringe on agriculture. He was assigned to the Bureau of Home Economics but loaned to the secretary's office as adviser on finance (5, p. 247). In 1935 he moved to the National Resources Committee as director of the Industrial Section (169, p. 352).

William I. Meyers of Cornell also served the Department in the thirties. He was named professor of farm finance at Cornell in 1920 and was granted a leave in 1933 to become assistant chairman of the Federal Farm Board (155, p. 497). In this position he was instrumental in bringing the federal land banks, the immediate credit banks, the joint stock land banks, and the cooperative loans of the Federal Farm Board into one bureau, the Farm Credit Administration (155, p. 497). He served as its Deputy Governor and later was named head of the Administration (120, p. 313; 139, p. 742). According to one author, he was the only professor to head a government unit during the first fourteen months of the New Deal (139, p. 742).

A professor of marketing at Cornell in the early twenties, Howard E. Babcock was added to the Department as assistant to the Chairman of the Farm Board (155, p. 497). Herman Oliphant had taught at Chicago,

Johns Hopkins, and elsewhere before coming to Washington as general counsel for the Federal Farm Board followed by service with the Farm Credit Administration (3, p. 62; 155, p. 497). Since many of the New Deal programs overlapped and were closely related, a person assigned to one agency often did work more related to another area. In Oliphant's case, he may have made his most significant contribution by suggesting a plan whereby the government could buy gold (169, p. 239). Working in Washington was not a new experience for Oliphant. While a professor at Johns Hopkins in the twenties, he assisted Senator George W. Norris and others in drafting a bill to protect labor (168, p. 114).

Calvin B. Hoover was attracted to government service after many years of teaching, most of them at Duke University. Hoover agreed to serve as an economic consultant in the Agricultural Adjustment Administration on a part-time basis. He accepted a government position because of the grave economic emergency that existed and hope that it would be a temporary arrangement, but he eventually obtained a leave of absence from Duke and moved to Washington (97, p. 174). When he became a consultant for the USDA, the problem of displaced agricultural laborers, sharecroppers, and tenants was attracting much attention and criticism. Since Hoover was the only economic adviser who lived in the South and had had experience as a dirt farmer, he was asked to make an economic analysis of the situation (97, p. 156). The report which he submitted was partially responsible for the Bankhead-Jones Act, which among other things provided for the Farm Security Administration (97, p. 158).

Hoover was also a member of the President's Drought Relief Committee and later, on the advice of John M. Keynes, became its secretary (97, pp. 160, 174). According to Hoover, Keynes declared, "If you want to have any real effect upon economic policy, you must take a responsible operating job" (97, p. 172). Hoover was named to a relatively minor position to succeed Frederic C. Howe (97, p. 165). Howe was somewhat out of place in the new administration. He had been a veteran of many liberal causes since the early 1900's and still had an unquenched hope at age sixty-six (169, p. 51). He approached Moley after the inauguration concerning the possibility of a government post. Howe's position in the Department of Agriculture was not ideal, and he was soon ousted in a policy struggle within the Department. (140, p. 128; 169, pp. 74, 79).

Carl D. Taylor became special assistant to the director of the Division of Subsistence Homesteads in 1933 after teaching at a number of schools as well as being dean of the Graduate School at North Carolina State from 1923 to 1932. In the thirties he also served in the Agricultural Adjustment Administration, the Resettlement Administration, and the Bureau of Agricultural Economics (29, p. 815). Another academician associated with resettlement was Will W. Alexander. He served as Tugwell's chief aid in the Resettlement Administration and became its Administrator when Tugwell resigned (5, p. 212; 169, p. 372). When the Farm Security Administration replaced the Resettlement Administration, Alexander became its first head (169, p. 381).

In November, 1933, Roosevelt appointed Ferdinand A. Silcox as Chief of the Forest Service. Silcox received a Master's degree from the Yale School of Forestry in 1905 when it was the terminal degree in the field. From 1905 to 1919 he was in the Forest Service and returned in 1933 (173, pp. 7-8). Roosevelt also consulted with Nelson C. Brown of the New York State College of Forestry regarding the use of unemployed in the forests (169, p. 337). These are but a few of the academicians in the USDA; some of the others are listed in the appendix.

State Department

The State Department gained more academicians than the two mentioned earlier, Moley and Berle. Secretary of State Hull retained Herbert Feis as Economic Adviser, and Stanley K. Hornbeck remained as head of the Division of Far Eastern Affairs (182, p. 313). Feis' influence in matters of policy appeared to have increased in the thirties. He played an important role in the American side of the London Economic Conference (169, pp. 200-28); and as a result of the reorganization of the Department in the thirties, he was designated adviser on international economic affairs (182, p. 330). In 1933 Francis B. Sayre, Woodrow Wilson's son-in-law, filled the vacated post of Assistant Secretary of State (182, p. 313). He was on the law faculty at Harvard from 1919 to 1934, but apparently was on leave much of the time because he worked for the Siamese Government on several occasions in the 1920's and early thirties (31, p. 977). Sayre's training and experience in international administration was excellent preparation for a position in the State Department. In 1939 he resigned to become high commissioner to the Philippine Islands (182, p. 313).

To implement the provisions of the act providing for reciprocal trade agreements, the Division of Trade Agreements was established in 1934 by the State Department. A man of wide experience and academic training was selected to head it. Henry F. Grady had a Ph. D. degree from Columbia, had taught at several schools, and had served as trade commissioner and commercial attaché abroad; in addition, he served in the Bureau of Foreign and Domestic Commerce (29, p. 317; 182, p. 318). When Sayre went to the Philippines, Grady was appointed Assistant Secretary of State (182, p. 336). In 1933 the Office of Historical Adviser was divided; Cyril Wynne was named chief of the Division of Research and Publication (182, p. 296), and E. Wilder Spaulding became assistnat chief (182, p. 317). In the thirties the Department of State created the Division of Cultural Relations to "cultivate closer cultural relations by the exchange of professors, teachers, and students, by the dissemination abroad of representative intellectual and cultural work of the United States, and to cooperate in the fields of music, art, literature, and other intellectual and cultural attainments" (182, p. 333). The head of the division was Ben M. Cherrington, a faculty member at the University of Denver and chairman of the Department of International Relations beginning in 1928 (29, p. 146).

A few academicians were appointed as ministers or ambassadors to foreign nations. Undoubtedly the most noted was William E. Dodd, professor of history at the University of Chicago. Dodd had a lengthy

association with the Democratic Party and had served the national
government during and after World War I. In the twenties he never entirely lost interest in politics, and in the early thirties he continued
to press for government positions for specialists (50, pp. 171-74). Filling the position of ambassador to Germany was one of the difficult personnel positions faced by Roosevelt. The rise of Hitler removed the
consideration of the wealthy campaign-contributor type because the situation required an able ambassador who could protect American interests and
intelligently report the political developments of the Nazi regime. After
offering the position to James M. Cox and considering several others,
Roosevelt offered the job to Dodd (182, p. 316). Dodd had a number of
characteristics that made him attractive to Roosevelt. He had strong ties
to the Wilson wing of the party, had taken an active part in the campaign
of 1932, and had a Ph. D. degree from Leipzig. Coupled with these features, he had a prominent reputation as a progressive historian, all of
which prompted Roosevelt to "herald his selection as the end of a care-
ful search for just the right man" (50, p. 190).

There were probably several reasons for Dodd's accepting the ambassadorship. He had wanted a position in Roosevelt's administration,
and problems in his department at Chicago must have made a change in
scenery attractive. In addition, Dodd "primarily saw the position as an
opportunity to help reverse the isolationist policy of the United States
--an achievement which Dodd considered both possible and vital to economic well-being in America and the world" (50, pp. 174, 190). A few
additional academicians are included in this section for illustrative

purposes, but this should not be interpreted as a complete list. John Lee Coulter, the academician on the Tariff Commission, was detached from it in 1933 to guide the preliminary work on a sugar agreement with Cuba (120, p. 223). In the latter part of the thirties the University of Chicago furnished two other academicians for government service. Robert Herrick became Government Secretary of the Virgin Islands and was succeeded by his colleague, Robert Morss Lovett. Both had many years service at Chicago; Lovett joined the Chicago faculty in 1893 (29, p. 509; 130, pp. 268-69), and Alvin H. Hansen joined the State Department in 1934 as an economist primarily responsible for trade agreements. He had taught at Brown University and the University of Minnesota (29, p. 346; 169, p. 257).

Other Departments and Agencies

Since so many academicians were engaged by the government only the more prominent ones are grouped together here; others are listed in the appendix. The Assistant Secretary of Commerce in Roosevelt's first Cabinet left the faculty at the University of Pennsylvania to take the position. John Dickinson received a Ph. D. degree at Harvard and then taught at four eastern schools before moving to Pennsylvania. After two years in Commerce, he became chairman of the Central Statistical Board and in 1935 was named Assistant United States Attorney General (29, p. 213). Dickinson was very active in the formative stages of several New Deal programs, especially those related to labor and industry (169, pp. 96-99).

Thurman W. Arnold, a lawyer and academician of some note, was attracted to government service during the New Deal. He was a lecturer on law at the University of Wyoming during the twenties, and then was dean of the College of Law at West Virginia University in the late twenties. Prior to joining the Agricultural Adjustment Administration, he was a professor at Yale. From the USDA he moved to the Securities and Exchange Commission as a trial examiner and then to the Department of Justice. By the late thirties he had been elevated to the post of Assistant Attorney General (29, p. 25).

The New Deal programs increased the need for people with a background similar to Isador Lubin's. Lubin had taught at the Universities of Missouri and Michigan and the Brookings Institution. He had served with several boards during World War I and was brought back to the government in 1933. He was made chief of the statistical division of the Bureau of Labor and served on the boards of a number of New Deal programs (29, p. 510).

In 1933, Edwin R. Embree of the Julius Rosenwald Fund expressed a concern for the treatment of blacks in the country. As a result, directors of the Fund encouraged the government to appoint a person to be responsible for the fair treatment of Negroes by agreeing to pay the individual's salary. The position was created in the Department of the Interior, and Clark Foreman, a young Georgian employed by the Fund, was appointed to the position (170, p. 432). Robert C. Weaver, who had an earned doctorate from Harvard, began his many years of government service as Foreman's assistant. When Foreman vacated the post, Weaver was named to succeed him (170, pp. 432-35).

Monetary Brain Trust

A study of this nature would be much more compact if each individual and each problem could be put in a particular category; however, this is always difficult to do and unusually so in the case of the New Deal. Committees and agencies had shifting and overlapping memberships and frequently a program involved more than one agency. Because of these factors, it is difficult to place some of the following academicians in specific categories, yet they played vital roles in formulating New Deal policies. A good designation for some of them could be the monetary brain trust. A leading member of this group was George F. Warren of Cornell. A consultant for the Agriculture Department in the twenties, Warren had built up a reputation as an expert in land use (5, pp. 107, 119; 169, p. 234). In the thirties, he received a great deal of attention for his views on dollar devaluation as outlined in the book Prices, co-authored by Warren and Frank A. Pearson, also of Cornell (12, p. 297). Roosevelt had known Warren for several years and was especially attracted to his ideas on gold purchase policy. There seems to be little question but that Warren's views greatly influenced the making of the decision to have the government purchase gold and to set the purchase price (169, pp. 235-41).

James Harvey Rogers, a Yale professor of economics and a former student of Irving Fisher's, was associated with Warren on the gold question. Although not in full agreement with the Warren thesis on the gold question, he served with Warren as a monetary adviser to Roosevelt. He had served on a national committee during Hoover's adminstration, so this was not his initial effort in government service; however, the opportunity to influence policy was much greater (159, p. 302; 169, pp. 235-36). The venerable Irving Fisher also influenced the thinking and planning on the monetary issues but took no active part in any of the discussions. He influenced thinking on the subject primarily through his book Stable Money, a History of the Movement, and he visited Hyde Park to talk with President Roosevelt (12, p. 297; 169, p. 235).

Another academician who served as an adviser on money questions was Oliver Mitchell Wentworth Sprague, a professor of Roosevelt's at Harvard (168, p. 323). Sprague had served as adviser to the Federal Reserve Bank in New York and in 1930 became adviser to the Bank of England (15, p. 7). Roosevelt called him home and sent him back to London as an adviser to the Treasury Department at the Economic Conference (140, p. 216). Among the others who influenced monetary policy were H. Parker Willis, Beardsley Ruml, and Leon Henderson. Willis was professor of banking at Columbia University but had a long association in the government and in the thirties aided in drafting new banking laws (155, p. 497). Ruml had worked in industry and foundations much of the time after receiving a Ph. D. degree at Chicago in 1917. In 1931 he became dean of the Social Sciences Division at the University of Chicago and served as an adviser in the New Deal (29, p. 713; 187, p. 446). Henderson will be discussed later.

A young academician whose influence grew after the first few years of the New Deal was Lauchlin Currie (170, p. 387). Currie earned a doctorate at Harvard and taught at Harvard and Tufts before entering government service. He began with the Treasury Department, then became assistant director of research and statistics for the Federal Reserve

System and by the late thirties was administrative assistant to the President (29, p. 189).

New Deal Ventures

The new programs and boards associated with the New Deal presented academicians with new opportunities for service. Many academicians had advocated national planning for years, and the New Deal offered an opportunity to put some of their theories into practice. The passage of the National Industrial Recovery Act and the establishment of the National Recovery Administration (NRA) opened up new positions for academicians. In 1934 Roosevelt appointed a National Industrial Recovery Board to administer NRA. Leon C. Marshall and Walton H. Hamilton were the academicians on the board (169, p. 157). Marshall had worked with labor and industrial policies during World War I and had been teaching since 1903. Most of his teaching experience had been at the University of Chicago and at Johns Hopkins University (29, p. 549).

Walton was on the faculty at Yale when he was named to the board, but he had held faculty appointments at the Universities of Texas, Michigan, Chicago, Amherst College and Brookings Institution (29, p. 343). In the thirties he was also a delegate to the International Labor Organization Conference in Geneva and special assistant to the United States Attorney General (31, p. 992). The renowned academician, Robert M. Hutchins, was suggested for chairman of the Board and operating head of NRA. Roosevelt and Hutchins were receptive to the idea, but a delay resulting from conflicting desires among Roosevelt's advisers caused Hutchins to end the negotiations when he requested that his name be removed from the list of those being considered (169, p. 157).

An early addition to the staff of NRA was Leon Henderson. Henderson, a statistician, taught at the Wharton School and the Carnegie Institute of Technology before joining the Russell Sage Foundation, where he was employed when he joined the NRA. He also served as an adviser to a Senate committee dealing with manufacturing and to the Works Progress Administration (WPA) and was appointed to the Securities and Exchange Commission in the late thirties (29, p. 369). Lindsey Rogers, a professor of government and public law at Columbia, served as a code-maker for the NRA. Rogers' success in mediating disputes was cited by some as an example of the neutral role that academicians could play (139, p. 746). After leaving the position of deputy administrator with NRA, Rogers became chairman of the Board of Labor Review of PWA (31, p. 996).

Leo Wolman was director of research for the Amalgamated Clothing Workers during the twenties and thirties, and at the same time he had considerable contact with Roosevelt. After becoming involved with Roosevelt during the campaign he continued the association in Washington. Wolman worked with the NRA, the National Labor Board, and the Automobile Labor Board. In the earlier years of the century, he had received a Ph. D. degree at Johns Hopkins, taught for about a decade, and worked with some of the boards created during World War I (29, p. 911). The NRA also utilized the services of W. H. Spencer, dean of the University of Chicago School of Commerce and Administration; Earle D. Howard, professor of economics at Northwestern; and Alexander Sachs (120, p. 314; 130, p. 214).

In addition to those mentioned, the WPA engaged many other academicians, some of whom are included in this section. One of the boards set
up within WPA was the National Planning Board, which was responsible for
keeping track of public works projects and for fitting them into national
planning (169, pp. 350, 384). Two of the three board members were aca-
demicians--Charles E. Merriam and Wesley C. Mitchell. In 1934 the designation was changed to the National Resources Board, and in 1935 it was
reorganized into the National Resources Committee (169, pp. 350-51).
Merriam and Mitchell had been members of Hoover's Committee on Recent
Social Trends, which had recommended resources planning (203, p. 15).
Other academicians previously mentioned but associated with WPA were
Gardiner Means, Lindsay Rogers, and Beardsley Ruml (31, p. 996; 169,
pp. 351-52). V. O. Key, Jr., had his first taste of government service
as a research technician with the National Resources Committee. He
taught at the University of California Los Angeles prior to joining the
Committee (31, p. 993).

As the government became more involved in labor disputes, the academic community was a prime source of agency members and of analysis and
consultants. When the National Labor Relations Board was established by
Roosevelt in 1934, Lloyd K. Garrison, dean of the Wisconsin Law School,
was appointed chairman (169, p. 151). When he resigned in 1935, J.Warren
Madden, professor of law at the University of Pittsburgh, succeeded him
as chairman (169, p. 406). An academician suited for the position by
virtue of experience and training, Harry A. Millis was appointed to the
board in 1934 and was later named chairman. Millis received a doctorate

at Chicago in 1899 and for nearly four decades was engaged in teaching, research, and public service (29, p. 574). William M. Leiserson's service in the Labor Department during World War I and his work in labor arbitration during the twenties, coupled with his knowledge of economics, made him an outstanding choice for labor boards in the thirties. From a professorship at Antioch College he moved to Washington, where he served the National Labor Relations Board, the National Mediation Board, and NRA (29, p. 488). Leon C. Marshall, mentioned earlier in connection with NRA, also served with the National Labor Board (29, p. 549), as did J. Mark Jacobson, professor of political science at the University of Wisconsin (31, p. 993).

Roosevelt appointed a cabinet-level Committee on Economic Security to make a study which eventually resulted in the Social Security program created by Congress (169, pp. 304-05). The research director for the study was Edwin E. Witte of the University of Wisconsin, and his colleague, Arthur J. Altmeyer, was chairman of the Technical Board on Economic Security (169, p. 304; 187, p. 337). President Frank P. Graham of the University of North Carolina aided the study by serving as chairman of an advisory group to the cabinet committee (29, p. 317).

The creation of the Tennessee Valley Authority tended to draw additional academicians into government service. The TVA board was composed of three members appointed by the President, and the first board included two college presidents, Arthur E. Morgan and Harcourt A. Morgan. Arthur Morgan became president of Antioch College in 1920 and his unique qualifications for membership on the TVA board were outlined by one authority on the New Deal: "Few American engineers had had so much experience with flood control projects, beginning with the famous Miami Conservancy District, which he designed before the First World War to prevent a recurrence of the Dayton flood" (169, p. 327). In addition to being chairman, Arthur Morgan was responsible for building dams and for developing planning and educational programs (170, p. 363). Harcourt Morgan was an agricultural scientist who had been dean of the College of Agriculture at the University of Tennessee and since 1919, president of the University (169, p. 328). He had promoted agricultural activities in the South for decades, so his responsibility on the board was to supervise agricultural activities and to produce and distribute fertilizers (170, p. 363).

Roosevelt also continued the practice of earlier presidents of appointing committees to study major national questions. In 1936 the Committee on Administrative Management was appointed to study administrative management in the government and to submit recommendations to the President (31, p. 995). Academicians on the committee were Charles E. Merriam, Louis Brownlow, and Luther Gulick. Brownlow was engaged in newspaper work from the beginning of the century, but in 1931 he became director of Public Administration for Clearing House and a lecturer at the University of Chicago (29, p. 108). Gulick received a Ph. D. degree at Columbia in 1920 and became a member of the faculty the following year (29, p. 330).

The Social Science Research Council appointed with Roosevelt's approval the Commission of Inquiry on Public Service Personnel. The Commission was to examine the problems of personnel in the nation and to outline a program for the future. Lotus D. Coffman, president of the

University of Minnesota, was Chairman, and Charles E. Merriam was on the Committee (31, p. 989). In 1936 the President appointed an Advisory Committee on Education with the charge to "study the existing program of Federal aid for vocational education, the relation of such training to general education, and the extent of the need for an expanded program" (31, p. 987). The chairman of the committee, Floyd W. Reeves, had a varied background in the field of education. He received a Ph.D. degree from the University of Chicago in 1925, after having served in the public schools of South Dakota and as professor at Transylvania College. After teaching four years at the University of Kentucky, he accepted a faculty position at the University of Chicago. In 1933 he became director of personnel for TVA and then accepted the chairmanship of the advisery committee (29, p. 680; 31, p. 996).

Regulatory Commissions

The number of academicians appointed by Roosevelt to the regulatory agencies in the first years of his administration was limited especially when compared with the number of academicians in other areas of government. William M. W. Splawn was appointed to the Interstate Commerce Commission in 1934 (90, p. 35). He had political contacts and excellent training and experience for the position. Splawn was president of the University of Texas and had served as dean of the Graduate School of the American University, which gave him an opportunity to develop administrative technique (90, p. 85). Experience as a member of the Texas Railroad Commission, as an arbitrator in labor disputes, and as special counsel to

the House Committee on Interstate and Foreign Commerce added significantly
to his qualification (90, p. 86).

George C. Mathews, a professor of public utilities at Northwestern
University, was appointed to the Federal Trade Commission (90, pp. 122,
131). After less than a year he moved to the newly-created Securities
and Exchange Commission (90, p. 132). Henry F. Grady (discussed earlier)
became vice-chairman of the United States Tariff Commission in the thirties (29, p. 317). Grady was joined on the Commission by Oscar B. Ryder,
an economist for the Commission since 1919 (29, p. 717).

An outstanding professor of political science and public administration at the University of Chicago was appointed to the Civil Service Commission in 1934, and in the same year he became a member of the Central
Statistical Board (31, p. 999). Leonard D. White received a doctorate
from Chicago and taught at Clark University and Dartmouth College before
joining the Chicago faculty. His previous governmental experience at
the federal level included work as an investigator for Hoover's Committee
on Recent Social Trends (29, p. 888). A fellow academician described
White as "one of the ablest and sanest of American political scientists,
our foremost student of problems of public administration in this field
--a man of brilliant insight, tact, and sound judgement" (61, p. 228).

The New Deal gave birth to an additional regulatory agency in 1934,
the Securities and Exchange Commission (SEC). One writer described the
SEC in the early years as a "glamour outfit," which easily attracted the
bright young graduates of the country's leading law schools (167, p. 84).
On the first five-member board, James M. Landis was the only academician.

Landis, a law professor at Harvard, had aided the Committee on Interstate and Foreign Commerce in framing the 1933 Securities Act and later served as a special advisor to the Federal Trade Commission (90, p. 58; 140, p. 180). When Joseph Kennedy resigned from the Commission, Landis was appointed Chairman (169, p. 469). William O. Douglas, a Yale Law School professor, was brought to Washington by Kennedy to make a study of bond-holder's protective committees for the Commission. He then became a commissioner and followed Landis as chairman of the Commission (3, pp.93-94). Later President Roosevelt appointed Douglas to the Supreme Court.

The foregoing are most of the prominent academicians who served in the New Deal. Many more had an active part of the New Deal and, as one noted historian suggested, "Throughout the land scholars who stayed at their desks talked, wrote, and lectured differently because of the new concern for the forgotten man and for neglected areas of work that might help solve his problems" (46, p. 19). During the early years of the New Deal the nation witnessed the partial culmination of a trend that had its beginnings in the late nineteenth century. The scope of this involvement was suggested by Ernest K. Lindley: "Probably never before in its history has the Federal Government found important roles for so many men of fertile and courageous minds" (120, p. 315). This participation by academicians in the governmental affairs of the nation revealed that a university could be a public service institution of the highest type and by so doing confirmed the position that many academicians had been attempting to prove since the late eighteen hundreds.

CHAPTER VI

SUMMARY AND CONCLUSIONS

The extent of the involvement of academicians in government service
in the early years of Franklin D. Roosevelt's administration was not merely one of the peak periods which had occurred through the years. From one
consideration it was a high point, but more significantly was the culmination of a development which had been in the making for decades. Academicians had been moving toward a public service posture since the post-Civil
War era, and many of them had been making a special effort to demonstrate
that there was not a dichotomy between theory and practice. As has been
shown in this study, the movement was not a smooth ascent, but it went
through several phases accentuated by extensive involvement during certain other periods.

Beginning with the post-Civil War period, it has been pointed out
that academicians failed to make an extensive contribution to the solution of problems in American society. In addition, the Civil War, unlike the two world wars of the twentieth century, did not enhance the
image of the academician. In addition, materialism and anti-intellectualism, which were strong forces in the period, caused many academicians
to seek out the comfort of an ivory tower. But at the same time a transformation was taking place in higher education which helped pave the way
for the events of the twentieth century.

The growth of the concept of public service and the development of the utilitarian outlook were noticeable trends of American higher education in this period. Interwoven with these developments was the expansion of state colleges and universities. The state institution flourished in the West and Mid-west, and it was in this section of the United States that the service idea was most apparent. The University of Wisconsin and the State of Wisconsin made the concept a reality in the early years of the present century. It is interesting to note that even though state universities were in the forefront of the public service movement when academicians began to be widely accepted by the federal government, many of them came from private schools in the East. Indeed, the two institutions most represented in the New Deal were Harvard and Columbia; however, the presence in government service of alumni from these institutions reflects the influence of some of President Roosevelt's advisers.

In considering the evolution of the service idea and the factors which influenced American Higher Education, Brubacher and Rudy noted the following characteristics:

> What distinguished the American idea of the higher learning from other modern conceptions of the university was not only its essential democracy, but even more its positive dedication to the service of an evolving dynamic, democratic community. To the English concept of the general culture of the educated gentleman and the German concept of scholarly research for its own sake, the American university added another dimension; namely, that higher education to justify its own existence should seek to serve actively the basic needs of American life (20, p. 394).

Essential in the development of the public service role of the academician were the changes brought about in the curricular realm in the late nineteenth century. The expansion of the elective approach in the curriculum and the decline of the classical approach contributed to the offering of more utility-oriented courses. The emergence of the scientist and the social scientist was also a significant element in the public service movement. The social sciences developed in the United States in the post-Civil War era and initially were influenced greatly by German professors; however, the American social scientist tended to be a pragmatist, while the German scholar was more of a historicist. The American was more successful in supplying a logical connection between thought and action than his German mentor had been.

Even though the social scientist was at the core of the academicians involved in government service in the twentieth century, the transition into this role was not as easy for the social scientist as for the applied scientist. The chemist, the geologist, the physicist, and other applied scientists could prove their work in the laboratory. By contrast, the social scientist worked in a more subjective realm and men in public office were reluctant to call upon him. It took a generation for the social scientist to be accepted, and the full acceptance did not occur until the New Deal. The curricular changes - especially the influence of the utilitarian approach - and the changes in society in the past century opened new vistas to persons in higher education.

By the close of the nineteenth century rhetoric in support of academic public service was being freely spouted by college presidents and others in reponsible positions in higher education. Such utterances were especially characteristic of men who represented state colleges and universities. On the other hand, it would be erroneous to leave the impression that the academic community was totally committed to the concept of public service. It has been pointed out by Laurence Veysey and others that by the opening of the twentieth century the academic conservatives, who were concerned about mental discipline and the classical approach in the curriculum, still had considerable influence. However, advocates of research and utilitarianism were firmly entrenched and were in a position to influence significantly the role of higher education in the present century. Another noteworthy change in American higher education at the turn of the century was in the realm of leadership. By the first decade of the twentieth century, most of the leaders of the post-Civil War era had passed from the scene. Many of their replacements supported a public service role for academicians. These changes, coupled with the acknowledgement by the larger society of the need for the services of academicians, provided additional opportunities for members of the academic community.

The following account from The Rise of American Civilization reflects some of the conditions which were prevalent in American life which gave academicians expanded opportunities for public service:

> In a word, cumulative forces, complex and interacting, were beating upon the accepted order of things. Almost too young to be called accepted that order itself was born, of an industrial transformation which touched every phase of life and labor; was indeed still in constant change under the drive of invention, technology, and capitalist ambition (9, p. 538).

This direction in national life was enhanced by the pursuits of two strong personalities in the White House, Theodore Roosevelt and Woodrow

Wilson. As society underwent a transformation and became more complex, more and more academicians brought their talents to bear on the solution of public problems. The most notable example of endeavors on the state level was the Wisconsin Idea in the early years of the twentieth century. University personnel were also beginning to work with state and federal agencies across the land in attempting to solve problems associated with the industrial economy and other features of American culture in the twentieth century.

When academic people began to consider going into public service, there were two basic routes which were open. The elective avenue was always open, or the desire to help in solving questions of public interest could be fulfilled by the academicians influencing decisions and policy through providing expert analysis and advice. With very few exceptions the latter course was selected at the state and national levels. Most authorities on the subject have pointed out that academicians have not pursued the elective route in great numbers. Even though the notables who attained elective offices-- Woodrow Wilson, Henry Cabot Lodge, Samuel Fess, Hiram Bingham, and others-- were relatively few in number, their quality of service was generally outstanding. Also, there have been few academicians in the present century who have attempted to make their influence felt through the political parties.

By far the largest number of academicians found opportunities for service in appointive positions: as members of commissions, agencies and similar bodies; and as experts working with commissions and agencies. It is obvious that an appointment to cabinet-level positions or to membership on regulatory commissions placed a person in a position of some influence; however, the number of academicians in such positions within the scope of this study was limited, especially at the cabinet level. The regulatory commissions came into vogue in the early part of this century, and academicians served on all of them in the period under consideration.

One of the significant points in this study is that the large majority of the academicians who came into government service in the first three and a half decades of this century served as analysts and experts in certain departments or agencies of the government. A number of authors have been interested in this role of the academician and have attempted to analyze it. Possibly the most frequently cited reason for academicians' being brought in as experts has been the absence in our system of civil servants such as can be found in many of the European countries. Although members of the academic world did not have an exclusive hold on the qualities needed by the government, colleges and universities certainly possessed one of the available reservoirs of such talent. Academicians also proved to be effective in the role of experts, and as a result the utilization of their talents expanded as society became more complex and as the needs of the government grew.

The acceptance of the service role of academicians can be attributed partly to the time in which it developed. One of the features of American life at the opening of the present century was the emergence of the Progressive Movement. It was manifested in many ways; it significantly influenced both government and education, and its development generally paralleled the expansion of the public service role of academicians.

Progressivism favored the establishment of regulatory and administrative bodies; this trend caused progressives to look to colleges and universities for experts to serve on the commissions and to function as analysts and advisers. The upshot of these developments in the early years of this century was that academicians were being drawn into governmental affairs on the basis of their usefulness. It is readily apparent from the articles that appeared in periodicals at the time that the public began to recognize the contribution which academicians were making to society.

The appreciation may also have resulted from changes which were noticeable in the quality of professors. All of these changes contributed to the expanding role of the academician and helped in building up to the point reached in the 1930's.

A brief summary of the first three decades of the twentieth century reveals the manner in which this buildup took place. As President of the United States, Theodore Roosevelt encouraged the trend toward public service of academicians. He developed a relatively close association with the academic world through his scholarship; and while serving in the White House, he frequently called on academicians for technical advice on a host of issues. Roosevelt made use of commissions to study certain aspects of American life, and these commissions generally utilized the expertise of academicians in carrying out their assignments. The use of academicians in scientific and technical bureaus was also expanded during Roosevelt's administration, and college and university personnel were beginning to find opportunities in many segments of government. The

Department of Agriculture was in the forefront of agencies employing
academicians. Overall, Theodore Roosevelt created an atmosphere in
Washington in which academicians felt more comfortable than at anytime
prior to his inauguration.

William Howard Taft cannot be classified as an academician as defined in this study, but he had a number of connections with the academic world prior to becoming President, and he was not opposed to the
government's utilization of the services of persons from institutions
of higher education. There is no indication that academicians brought
into government service by Theodore Roosevelt felt uncomfortable because
of President Taft's policies. As a matter of fact, he was responsible
for additional academicians entering government service. The first member of a regulatory commission to have an earned doctorate was appointed
by President Taft. Academicians found opportunities for service in many
governmental agencies; however, men from the scientific fields continued
to be called on more frequently than their colleagues in less technical
fields. The number of academicians in the Congress increased slightly
during the early years of the present century, and the members of Congress began to rely more heavily on personnel from higher education for
conducting studies and as sources of information.

The election of Woodrow Wilson as President of the United States in
1912 may have appeared to some to have been the ultimate in the involvement of academicians in the operation of the national government. This
was the first and the only time in the history of the United States that
a person with an earned doctorate has been elected to the highest office

in the nation. Wilson's use of academicians was not as extensive as may have been expected, especially during the years preceding the war.

Wilson contributed to the development of an atmosphere in the national government in which academicians felt comfortable. David F. Houston, the first person with a doctorate to occupy a seat in the cabinet in the present century, was appointed Secretary of Agriculture, and other people from higher education were appointed to commissions and used in many facets of government service. The Department of Agriculture expanded its use of academicians, and President Wilson asked a number of professors to represent the United States in foreign countries. Academicians continued to find opportunities as experts, especially in the monetary and banking fields. The questions facing the nation in the early 1900's were of such a nature that social scientists, particularly economists, found many openings in government. The opportunities for social scientists were enhanced by the creation of the Federal Reserve System, the Federal Trade Commission, and other federal agencies. It is apparent that the number of academicians in government service increased steadily from the administration of President Theodore Roosevelt through the pre-war years of President Wilson's administration; however, this increase was small compared with the numerous opportunities provided as a result of the entry of the United States into World War I.

World War I was undoubtedly the most influential factor to that point in the history of the United States in attracting academicians into government service. The government officials seemed to turn almost instinctively to colleges and universities in looking for the necessary manpower

when the United States entered the war. Numerous academicians were involved in the war effort, and their contributions were not limited to a
few specialized areas. In addition to serving in the various branches
of the military forces, large numbers of academic personnel found positions in practically every agency of the government, and many others
contributed their talents on a part-time basis while maintaining their
faculty status.

Probably of greater significance than the number involved was the
impact of the war-related events on the image of the academicians in the
minds of many of the people in the nation. The breach between the practical and the theoretical was narrowed by the fact that the government
turned to colleges and universities in this time of need and by the ver-
satility and effectiveness which characterized the performance of academicians. It is apparent from the articles published by the leading literary
magazines of the time that the contribution of academicians went a long
way toward dispelling the stereotyped ideas which had haunted them for
years. Academicians proved to be competent in a number of fields; and,
probably to the surprise of many, they were able to work with individuals
from every profession and business.

Another important effect of the war and the peace negotiations was
the expansion of opportunities for the social scientists. The boards and
agencies created prior to the war increased the need for political scientists and economists, but during the war and immediately thereafter, both
groups were called upon to advise and aid the government on a host of
topics. A final effect of the war was that many of the academicians

remained in government service to assist with the problems at the end of the war and others elected to continue on a more permanent basis.

Academicians were again called upon when the United States government began to collect information and material for the peace negotiations. The group, known as Inquiry, was brought together to make preparations for the peace conference. It included a large number of academicians, headed by Sidney E. Mezes, who at the time was president of City College of New York. This use of academicians is another illustration of where the absence of a large number of professionals in government agencies made it necessary for the government to look elsewhere for assistance; and the academic community had the resources.

The academicians who served with the Inquiry included many of the country's most respected scholars. Those with expertise in history, geography and economics were especially valuable to the work of the Inquiry. The final report of the group was used by President Wilson in formulating the Fourteen Points. Academicians were not limited to preliminary work, but a number of them were included in the group which Wilson took to Paris. Academicians were not at the top level of negotiations, but they made a valuable contribution to the finished document. It is generally agreed that the reputation of academicians was enhanced by their work in connection with the peace; however, many college and university personnel became disillusioned by the outcome of the war and the ensuing peace, and as a result there was a feeling on the part of many that they should confine their activities to college campuses.

The period of the twenties is very significant as one studies the role of the academician in government service. As a result of the Progressive Movement, the war, an academician in the White House, and other factors, the number of academicians in government service increased greatly between the opening of the twentieth century and the termination of the administration of Woodrow Wilson. When the decade of the twenties opened, academicians were serving in many government agencies and departments. On the other hand, the period between the inauguration of Warren G. Harding and the inauguration of Franklin D. Roosevelt is frequently considered a time during which academicians were not found in government service. It was not a period in which there was a mass movement of scholars into government service, but by the same token there was not an exodus from government positions by academicians. The number of college and university personnel in government service leveled off during the twenties, and it can be viewed as an interim between the two peaks--World War I and the New Deal.

Contrary to the views of some writers, academicians continued to move into government positions even though the rate was not as rapid as it had been in other periods. The Department of Agriculture continued to develop programs which created a demand for the services of academicians, and the spade work for some of the Department's programs of the 1930's was done in the late twenties. Under the leadership of Secretary Herbert Hoover, the Department of Commerce made greater use of academicians in the twenties than it had prior to the war. Other departments, agencies, and commissions continued their use of academicians; and a representative from the academic community was in the cabinet during the administration of Presidents Harding, Coolidge, and Hoover.

There is at least one other development in the twenties which needs to be considered. The movements for social, political, and other reforms diminished in the twenties, but partly through the efforts of academicians, the desire for reforms remained alive and came to fruition in the thirties. The academicians became more involved and more active during the administration of President Hoover than they had been during the early years of the 1920's, and as a result the Hoover years served as a good springboard in the thirties for persons from colleges and universities who were interested in assisting the government.

The ultimate in the involvement of academicians in government service within the scope of this study was reached during the New Deal. Academicians reached new pinnacles during this period as a result of the increase in the number of participants and the types of positions offered to them. There has been much discussion of the reasons for President Roosevelt's turning to this group for assistance. One of the most widely accepted reasons is that the nation was in a crisis; and, as in other crucial periods, notably World War I, the government turned to college campuses for assistance. Roosevelt may have felt that it would have been unwise to rely too heavily on the businessmen, industrialists, and political leaders, who had been the dominant figures in the government in the twenties. The prevailing attitude of the American people toward these groups was not very favorable in the early 1930's.

The extensive use of academicians by Roosevelt may also be viewed as a logical extension of his practices as Governor of New York and as a

continuation of his use of personnel from higher education during the
campaign of 1932. The new ventures entered into by the government such
as Agricultural Adjustment, the Social Security programs, and the Tennessee Valley Authority increased the complexity of government and required
men of training and imagination. The college campus was one of the obvious places to look for personnel to assist in planning and implementing
new programs. In this regard, Curti commented: "In the depression of the
1930's, intellectuals found fresh opportunities for contributing their
specialized knowledge and training to the public weal" (45, p. 82).

It has been stated previously that the lack of trained civil servants
in the United States has caused Presidents to turn to other groups, and
this again was apparent during the early years of the New Deal. The following statement indicates the view of one writer regarding some of the
groups available to President Roosevelt: "Politicians could not handle
the issues raised by the depression; civil servants of the right type did
not exist to cope with them; and most business leaders seemed worse than
useless" (94, p. 214). It has also been suggested that the domination of
the national government from 1921 to 1933 by Republicans presented Roosevelt with a situation in which the number of democrats with experience in
government was very limited. Consequently, he had to seek assistance from
a number of quarters. Regardless of the reason or reasons for the decision by President Roosevelt to rely heavily on personnel from higher education, academicians were a vibrant part of his administration, and as
the New Deal programs were developed the need for such people accelerated.

In considering the involvement of academicians during the New Deal,
one can note the nature of their service. According to magazine and news

articles of the time, it is apparent that many Americans misunderstood the role played by academicians. One of the prevalent views was that Roosevelt had turned the government over to professors and that they were using it as a laboratory for trying untested theories and ideas. Academicians were being used more extensively than during any previous time in the history of the nation, and they did play a greater role in policy-making and in the administration of the government. However, the idea that a clique of professors was telling the President how to run the government is totally false. Businessmen, financiers, politicians and other groups, along with academicians, contributed to the decisions that were made.

Determining the factors responsible for the actions of a particular group is extremely difficult, particularly in the case of academicians in the New Deal. They undoubtedly were all not attracted to government service for the same reason. It is important to note that many of the academic New Dealers had a selfish interest in accepting positions in government service. Tugwell, Moley, Berle, and other advocates of planning viewed this as an opportunity to lay out a plan for the nation to follow in its development. Some academicians saw this as a chance to get changes made within a department or agency of government, while others thought they could chart the course which the world should follow in a particular field. To state that the academicians who came into government during the early 1930's were not interested in financial and political rewards would be misrepresenting the case. However, the academicians Roosevelt selected for the top positions, and many others, had as their primary concern the establishment of a system which would be the best for the country. The opportunity to aid in the planning and policy making was in keeping with the concept of public service which had continued as a strong element in American higher education.

Academicians were not as well accepted by the public during this period as they had been during World War I; but there was a difference in the nature of the crisis, and the press was much more skeptical regarding the influence of the brain trusters. The press was generally inclined to give Roosevelt a fair chance in the early years of his administration; however, as writers began to criticize programs they tended to direct their attack at the President's associates. The professors were good targets, and making fun of professors involved with practical affairs had become a common practice in American life (179, p. 227). In addition, the economic difficulties continued for a number of years, and many of the unsuccessful solutions were attributed to the professors.

Overall, the academicians made a significant contribution to the New Deal and to the public service concept. Their influence was seen most clearly in the areas of program development and implementation and in serving as advisers to the President. It is important to note that the academicians were not greatly involved with the political party organizations and that their influence was not felt to any extent in the political decisions of the New Deal. In fact, Moley's split with President Roosevelt probably grew out of a situation in which the President realized that Moley was more expendible than a valued member of the Democratic Party.

There were a few academicians whose relations with the President were such that they had a profound influence on the overall policy of

Roosevelt's administration. The most noted of this group were Raymond Moley, Adolf A. Berle, Rexford G. Tugwell, and Felix Frankfurter. However, it may be that those whose actions have had the greatest effect upon the course of events were the academicians who worked within an agency or department or in some specialized area. As was true for the entire period covered in this study, the Department of Agriculture exceeded other departments in using academicians. Personnel from higher education had been attracted to the Department since the latter part of the nineteenth century, but the influence of the academicians during the New Deal far exceeded their influence during any other period. Even though the Department was not headed by an academician, as had been true at other times, Tugwell, who was named assistant secretary, came to the position from a college campus, as did a number of other staff members. Milbern L. Wilson, L. C. Gray, Mordecai Ezekiel, Louis Bean, Gardner Means, and William I. Meyers joined other academicians in helping to initiate a number of economic and social reforms carried out through the Department of Agriculture.

Because of the economic problems of the 1930's, a number of academicians with expertise in the financial and monetary fields were called upon by President Roosevelt. This number included George F. Warren, James Harvey Rogers, M. W. Sprague, H. Parker Willis and others whose advice was sought on the grave economic issues which the nation faced in the decade.

Academicians were also invited to serve on many of the boards and commissions which had come into existence in the 1930's. The Tennessee

Valley Authority was administered by a three-member board, and the original board included two college presidents, Arthur E. Morgan and Harcourt
A. Morgan. The program of the Tennessee Valley Authority caused controversies in the nation and the board members were criticized by the oppo-
nents of TVA, but the two Morgans provided outstanding leadership.
Academicians were also selected by President Roosevelt to serve on the
Regulatory Commissions. The President continued the practice of appointing committees to study major national questions, and in the 1930's
committees were appointed to study administrative management in government, personnel problems in the nation, and national economic security.
Included in the membership of each of these committees were some of the
most respected academicians in the land.

As has been demonstrated in this study, academicians made a vital
contribution to the nation in the early thirties by providing ideas and
manpower needed by President Roosevelt. More important from a long-range
viewpoint is the impact that their contribution had on American thought.
The quality of their performance helped to dispel the stereotype of the
woolly-minded professors who were unable to separate theory and practice.
Lawyers had at one time served as the intellectual workhorses of government; but as national problems became more complex and required solutions
which could be provided by scientists, sociologists, economists, and
others from higher education, the role of the workhorse began to be
filled by academicians.

As one reflects on the early years of the New Deal, it becomes readily apparent that the academicians did not lead the nation astray. From

the vantage point of the mid-twentieth century, Bernard Sternsher made

the following observation:

> Fortunately, in the early 1960's, the public response
> to the employment of professors in government was far
> more favorable than it was in the 1930's. Perhaps the
> public recognized in calm retrospect, while heaving a
> retroactive sigh of relief, that Roosevelt's academic
> advisers were not the irresponsible screwballs depicted
> in the newspapers. Perhaps this change was due to a
> rise in the educational level of the population. Per-
> haps it was the result of a pendulum--like reaction
> rather than an evolutionary development (179, p. 409).

One other important "perhaps" is that it became apparent that cer-

tain types of expertise possessed by some members of the academic com-

munity were needed by the government. A. A. Berle emphasized this point

in an article published in 1961, when he stated that it would be "almost

unthinkable" for the government not to have several first-rate professors

of economics (13, p. 84). As has been emphasized throughout this study,

the involvement by academicians during the New Deal was the culmination

of a trend that had been under way in the United States for decades.

There is more evidence that it was an evolutionary development rather

than the swinging of a pendulum, as suggested by Sternsher.

It is obvious that a number of other points could be added to the

study of the academicians in government service. One of these relates

to the viewing of the New Deal as a culmination of public service by

academicians. Since their involvement reached new heights during and

following World War II, a study of government service by academicians

during the last three decades would be beneficial. In more recent years

the involvement of personnel from higher education in the business com-

munity has been studied by scholars, but relatively little attention has

been devoted to the study of the contributions made by academicians to
foreign countries. In the period since World War I, many prominent members of the academic community have aided countries throughout the world.

Another interesting aspect of the study of the academician in government service related to the positions held following government service.
Those who were successful in governmental roles frequently found lucrative
jobs being offered to them. When Harvey Wiley resigned as Chief Chemist
in the Department of Agriculture in 1912, he was offered a position with
Good Housekeeping at $125,000 per year (206, p. 320). Large numbers of
academicians returned to college and university campuses, but some never
got back to their campuses and enjoyed astonishing success in private
life.

It is acknowledged that not all aspects of the involvement of academi
cians in government service in the proposed time span have been explored,
but the extent of the involvement has been sufficiently established to
show a continuous trend from the late nineteenth century through the
early years of the New Deal. The trend was not a steady upswing, but it
developed in peak periods and conversely included at least one long
period of more limited involvement. However, with the involvement permitted by the New Deal, academicians had reached new heights of service.
American colleges and universities had realized at least a few of the
ideals for which they had been striving in the area of public service.
They had contributed significantly to the advancement of the nation
through the use of their professional training, and the quality of the
service rendered by academicians was such that those who followed could
expect to be invited to serve in responsible positions in the government.

APPENDICES

171

APPENDIX A

ADDITIONAL ACADEMICIANS ASSOCIATED WITH WORLD WAR I

The following academicians were associated with the government during the War or during the years immediately thereafter. The name is
followed by the governmental body which the individual was associated
and the specialty of the academician.

E. E. Agger - Federal Reserve Board - Economics
George H. Allen - U. S. Army - Philology
Frederic B. Artz - U. S. Army - European History
George Merrick Baker - U. S. Army - German Language
Charles H. Beeson- U. S. Army - Philology
James Washington Bell - U. S. Army - Finance
Abraham Berglund - Tariff Commission - Economics
Joseph Walter Bingham - War Trade Board - Law
Francis H. Bird - U. S. Army, War Labor Board - Economics
Roy G. Blakey - War Trade Board - Public Finance
Ralph H. Blanchard - U. S. Army, Shipping Board - Insurance
Paul F. Bloomhardt - U. S. Navy - History
Ernest L. Bogart - War Trade Board - Economic History
Clarence D. Brenner - U. S. Army - French Literature
Philo Melvin Buck - U. S. Army - Comparative Literature
Walter Stanley Campbell - U. S. Army - English Literature
Samuel P. Capen - Council National Defense, War Department -
                        Education
Dean Neil Carothers - U. S. Army, State Department - Economics
William S. Carpenter - U. S. Army - Political Science
George Carver - U. S. Army - English Literature
Arthur Cleveland - Department of Labor - Drama
Charles C. Colby - Shipping Board - Geography
Arthur H. Cole - U. S. Army - Economic History
Wilson Compton - Emergency Fleet Corporation - Economics
Walter W. S. Cook - U. S. Army - Archeology
Melvin T. Copeland - Council National Defense, War Industry
                        Board - Economics
John H. Cover - Food Administration - Economics
Ira B. Cross - War Industry Board - Economics
Tom Peete Cross - U. S. Army - Celtic Languages and Literature
Stuart Daggett - War Industry Board - Economics
H. W. Davis - Food Administration - English
Arthur L. Day - War Industry Board - Geophysics

172

Edmund Ezra Day - Shipping Board, War Industry Board - Economics
J. Anton de Haas - U. S. Army - International Relations
Frank H. Dixon - Shipping Board - Economics
John Donaldson - Shipping Board , State Department - International
           Economics
Paul H. Douglas - Emergency Fleet Corporation - Economics
Horace B. Drury - Shipping Board - Economics
Charles E. Dunbar, Jr. - U. S. Army - Law
C. S. Duncan - Shipping Board - Economics
Lynn R. Edminster - U. S. Army, Shipping Board, Tariff Commission -
           Economics
George Wicker Elderkin - U. S. Army - Archeology
John Erskine - U. S. Army - English Literature
John A. Fairlie - War Department - Political Science
Harold U. Faulkner - U. S. Army - American History
F. B. Garver - Shipping Board - Economics
Julius Goebel, Jr. - U. S. Army - International Law
Henry F. Grady - Shipping Board - Economics
Kent Roberts Greenfield - U. S. Army - Modern European History
Clare Elmer Griffin - U. S. Army, Shipping Board - Economics
Clyde L. Grose - U. S. Army - English, History
George C. Haas - State Department - Oriental Philology
J. E. Hagerty - Food Administration - Social Work
Ernest H. Hahne - U. S. Army - Public Finance
Robert Murray Haig - Treasury Department - Political Economy
William T. Ham - Agriculture Department - Economics
W. Scott Hastings - U. S. Army - French Literature
J. R. Hayden - U. S. Army - Government & Politics
Carlton J. H. Hayes - U. S. Army - Modern European History
H. C. Heaton - U. S. Army - Romance Languages
W. W. Hill - State Department - Anthropology
Henry G. Hodges - Emergency Fleet Corporation - Political Science
Edwin Hopkins - Bureau of Education - English
Willard E. Hotchkiss - War Labor Board - Economics
Manley O. Hudson - Labor Department - International Law
Grover G. Huebner - War Trade Board, Federal Trade Commission -
           Transportation
Ralph G. Hurlin - U. S. Army - Social Research
S. B. Hustredt - U. S. Army - English Literature
Carl W. Johnson - U. S. Army - German Literature
Emory R. Johnson - Shipping Board, War Trade Board - Transportation
           Commerce
T. F. Jones - U. S. Navy - History
Charles H. Judd - Food Administration - Education, Educational
           Psychology
E. M. Kayden - War Trade Board - Economics
Edwin R. Keedy - U. S. Army - Law
Truman L. Kelley - U. S. Army - Statistics

Carl Kelsey - War Risk Insurance - Sociology
Frederic E. Lee - State Department - Economics
Isador Lubin - Food Administration, War Industry Board, War
            Trade Board - Economics
Leverett S. Lyon - Food Administration - Economics
Kemp Malone - U. S. Army - English Philology
Milo R. Maltbie - Shipping Board, War Industry Board - Municipal
            Government
L. C. Marshall - Council National Defense, Emergency Fleet
            Corporation, War Labor Policies Board -
            Economics, Administration
Charles E. Martin - War Trade Board, Food Administration -
            International Law and Relations
Ernest Whitney Martin - U. S. Army - Classics
Harold D. Meyer - U. S. Army - Sociology
Frederick C. Mills - U. S. Army - Economics
Samuel Eliot Morison - U. S. Army, Paris Peace Conference - History
F. R. Moulton - U. S. Army - Mathematics
Bruce D. Mudgett- War Trade Board - Economics, Statistics
Dana G. Munro - U. S. Army - Latin American History
Wallace Notestein - Committee on Public Information, State
            Department, Paris Peace Conference - English,
            History
William F. Ogburn - National War Labor Board, Bureau of Labor
            Statistics - Sociology
Sidney R. Packard - U. S. Army - Medieval History
Curtis Hidden Page - U. S. Army - Literature
W. A. Paton - War Trade Board - Accounting
O. K. Patton - U. S. Army - Law
Frederic L. Paxson - U. S. Army - American History
Dexter Perkins - U. S. Army - American Diplomatic History
Ralph Barton Perry - U. S. Army - Philosophy
Charles Edward Person - U. S. Army - Economics
Walter W. Pettit - U. S. Army, Paris Peace Conference - Sociology
Robert S. Platt - U. S. Army - Geography
Joseph E. Pogue - Fuel Administration - Geology
Allen W. Porterfield - U. S. Army - German
F. W. Powell - War Trade Board - Political Science
William K. Prentice - U. S. Army - Ancient History
J. G. Randall - Shipping Board - History
John Crowe Ransom - U. S. Army - English
J. F. Raschen - U. S. Army - Modern Languages
Harold L. Reed - U. S. Army - Economics
Lowell J. Reed - War Trade Board - Mathematical Statistics
Carlton C. Rice - Post Office, War Risk Insurance - Romance
            Linguistics
Robert Riegel - U. S. Navy - Statistics
T. W. Riker - U. S. Army - History

Daniel S. Robinson- U. S. Navy - Philosophy
Robert K. Root - U. S. Army - English Literature
Leo S. Rowe - Treasury Department, State Department - Government
C. O. Ruggles - Shipping Board - Economics
Howard J. Savage - U. S. Army - English Philology
Bernadotte E. Schmitt - U. S. Army- European History
Robert Scoon - U. S. Army - Greek Philosophy
Horace Secrist - Shipping Board - Economics
Edward H. Sirich - U. S. Army - French Literature
Sumner H. Slichter - U. S. Army - Economics
J. Russell Smith - War Trade Board - Economic Geography
Mark A. Smith - Tariff Commission - Economics
T. V. Smith - U. S. Army - Philosophy
M. Lyle Spencer - U. S. Army - Journalism
N. I. Stone - U. S. Army - Economics
J. W. Swain - U. S. Army - Ancient History
T. W. Van Metre - Shipping Board - Economics
Jacob Viner - Shipping Board - Economics
Stephen S. Visher - Geological Survey, Agriculture Department -
                    Social Geography
Henry F. Walradt - War Trade Board - Public Finance
Matthew J. Walsh - U. S. Army - Medieval History
W. S. Webb - U. S. Army - Archeology
Leo Wolman - War Industry Board, Council National Defense - Economics
Robert M. Woodbury - Labor Department - Labor Statistics
Erville B. Woods - National War Labor Board - Sociology
Erich W. Zimmermann - Bureau of Mines - Economics
George F. Zook - Treasury Department, Council National Defense -
                 History

APPENDIX B

ADDITIONAL ACADEMICIANS ASSOCIATED WITH THE NEW DEAL

The following is a list of academicians who served in government positions in the early years of the New Deal but who are not included in the body of the chapter. The governmental body with which each was associated and the specialty of the academician are also included.

Lewis W. Abbott - National Labor Relations Board - Economics, Sociology
Don S. Anderson - Agricultural Adjustment Administration - Agricultural Economics
Wilhelm Anderson - Bureau of Agricultural Economics - Social Philosophy
George B. L. Arner - Agricultural Adjustment Administration - Agricultural Trade
Theodore N. Beckman - Department of Commerce, Federal Trade Commission - Economics
A. G. Black - Bureau of Agricultural Economics, Farm Credit Administration - Agricultural Economics
Roy G. Blakey - Department of Agriculture, Department of Commerce - Public Finance
Ralph H. Blanchard - Social Security Board, Securities and Exchange Commission - Insurance
Roy Blough - Federal Emergency Relief Administration, Social Security Board, Treasury Department - Economics
Phillips Bradley - Department of Agriculture, Immigration and Naturalization Service - Political Science
J. Douglas Brown - Social Security Board - Economics
Eugene W. Burgess - Agricultural Adjustment Administration, National Recovery Administration - Economics
Eveline M. Burns - Works Progress Administration, Treasury Department, Federal Reserve Board, Social Security Board - Economics
Roy J. Burroughs - Federal Housing Administration - Economics
S. McClellan Butt - National Recovery Administration, Department of Labor - Philosophy, Economics
Robert D. Calkins - Agricultural Adjustment Administration, National Recovery Administration, Bureau of Reclamation - Economics
David F. Cavers - Department of Agriculture, Justice Department - Regulatory Law

176

Charlton F. Chute - Public Works Administration - Government
              Administration
Jane Perry Clark - Social Security Board - Government
John M. Clark - National Planning Board, National Recovery
              Administration - Economics
John H. Cover - Federal Emergency Relief Adminstration, Bureau
              Labor Statistics - Economics
Albert E. Croft - Employment Service - Sociology
Harry Lewis Custard - Federal Home Loan Bank Board - Philosophy
Arthur Dahlberg - National Recovery Administration, Department of
              Commerce, Works Progress Administration - Economics
Carroll R. Daugherty - National Recovery Administration - Labor
              Economics
Charles M. Davis - Biological Survey - Geography
Arthur L. Day - Resources Planning Board - Geophysics
Prentice N. Dean - Tariff Commission - Economics
W. Edwards Deming - Department of Agriculture - Mathematics
Ralph L. Dewey - Department of Commerce, Department of Agriculture -
              Economics
J. Frederic Dewhurst - National Recovery Administration - Economics
Marshall E. Dimock - War Department, Department of Labor - Political
              Science
Linden S. Dodson - Department of Agriculture - Sociology
Richard P. Doherty - National Recovery Administration - Economics
John Donaldson - Foreign Trade - International Economics
Paul H. Douglas - National Recovery Administration, Social
              Security Board - Economics
Noel T. Dowling - Agricultural Adjustment Administration, Tennessee
              Valley Authority - Law
Horace B. Drury - National Recovery Administration - Economics
Edward A. Duddy - Department of Agriculture, Department of Interior
              - Economics
Halbert L. Dunn - Bureau of Statistics - Statistics
Lawrence L. Durisch - Tennessee Valley Authority - Public Administra-
              tion
László Ecker-Rácz - Treasury Department - Economics
A. Ross Eckler - Works Progress Administration, Census Bureau -
              Economics
Lynn R. Edminster - Agricultural Adjustment Administration, State
              Department - Economics
Martha M. Eliot - Department of Labor - Pediatrics
P. T. Ellsworth - Treasury Department - Economics
N. H. Engle - Department of Commerce - Economics
Ernest J. Engquist - Farm Credit Administration, Bureau of Agricul-
              tural Economics - Marketing
John B. Ewing - Social Security Board - Economics
Wirth F. Ferger - Department of Agriculture - Economics, Statistics
Waldo E. Fisher - National Recovery Administration - Industrial
              Relations

Percy Scott Flippin - National Recovery Administration, National
            Archives - American History
Robert S. Ford - Agricultural Adjustment Administration - Economics,
            Government
Herbert F. Fraser - National Recovery Administration, State
            Department - Economics
A. Anton Friedrich - National Recovery Administration - Economic
            Theory
William C. Frierson - Department of Labor - English
F. P. Gaines - Federal Emergency Relief Administration - English
John K. Galbraith - Department of Agriculture - Economics
George B. Galloway - National Recovery Administration, National
            Planning Association - Economics, Government
C. G. Garman - Farm Credit Administration - Agricultural Economics
James E. Gates - National Recovery Administration, Federal Power
            Administration - Economics
Arthur D. Thomas Gayer - Public Works Administration, National
            Resources Planning Board - Economics
Raymond W. Goldsmith - Securities and Exchange Commission -
            Economics
J. S. Gould - National Recovery Administration- Economics
Otto E. Guthe - Tennessee Valley Authority, Soil Conservation
            Service - Geography
Francis J. Haas - National Recovery Administration, National Labor
            Board, Works Progress Administration - Labor
            Economics
Ernest H. Hahne - National Recovery Administration, Works Progress
            Administration - Public Finance
Robert Murray Haig - National Resources Committee - Political Economy
Ford Poulton Hall - Employment Service - Government and Business
William T. Ham - Agricultural Adjustment Administration, Bureau of
            Agricultural Economics - Economics
Walton H. Hamilton - National Recovery Administration, Social
            Security Board - Economics, Law
Alvin H. Hansen - State Department, Social Security Board - Economics
Alice C. Hanson - Bureau of Labor Statistics - Social Economics
H. G. Hayes - Bureau of Foreign and Domestic Commerce - Economics
Edith F. Helman - Federal Deposit Insurance Corporation - Spanish
W. W. Hill - National Archives - Anthropology
A. F. Hinrichs - Bureau of Labor Statistics - Economics
Forrest R. Holdcamper - Civil Service Commission, National Archives
            - History
John A. Hopkins, Jr. - Works Progress Administration - Agricultural
            Economics
Roman L. Horne - Department of Agriculture, Works Progress Administra-
            tion, Federal Reserve Board - Economics
Donald C. Horton - Department of Commerce, Bureau of Agricultural
            Economics - Economics
Willard E. Hotchkiss - National Recovery Administration - Economics,
            Political Science

Homer Hoyt - Federal Housing Administration - Economics
G. Donald Hudson - Tennessee Valley Authority - Geography
Grover G. Huebner - Maritime Commission - Transportation
Ralph G. Hurlin - Federal Emergency Relief Administration, Social
                 Security Board - Social Research
Clifford L. James - Tariff Commission - Economics
James M. Jarrett - Tariff Commission - Economics
Sherman E. Johnson - Department of Agriculture - Agricultural
                 Economics
A.D.H. Kaplan - Bureau of Labor Statistics, Social Security Board
                 - Economics
Dexter M. Keezer - National Recovery Administration - Economics
M. Slade Kendrick - Agricultural Adjustment Administration - Public
                 Finance
Joseph G. Knapp - Department of Agriculture - Agricultural Economics
Leslie Alice Koempel - Department of Labor - Sociology
John H. Kolb - Federal Emergency Relief Administration - Rural
                 Sociology
Carl F. Kraenzel - Federal Emergency Relief Administration - Rural
                 Sociology
Theodore J. Kreps - Works Progress Administration, Maritime Commis-
                 sion - Economics
C. A. Kulp - Social Security Board - Insurance
Simon Kuznets - Departments of Commerce and Treasury - Economics,
                 Statistics
Simeon E. Leland - Treasury Department, National Resources Committee,
                 Tennessee Valley Authority - Economics
Albert Lepawsky - Department of Commerce, National Resources Plan-
                 ning Board - Political Science
Ben W. Lewis - National Recovery Administration - Economics
Forrest E. Linder - Census Bureau - Demography, Vital Statistics
C. E. Lively - Federal Emergency Relief Administration, Department
                 of Agriculture - Sociology
D. Philip Locklin - Interstate Commerce Commission, Maritime Commis-
                 sion - Economics
Charles P. Loomis - Department of Agriculture - Sociology
Leslie Lovass - Tariff Commission - Economics
George A. Lundberg - Federal Emergency Relief Administration -
                 Sociology, Statistics
Leverett S. Lyon - National Recovery Administration - Economics
John W. McBride - National Recovery Administration, Bureau of Labor
                 Statistics - Economics
William D. McCain - National Archives - Archives
Thomas C. McCormick - Works Progress Administration - Sociology
K. C. McMurry - Department of Agriculture, National Resources Plan-
                 ning Board - Geography
Roswell Magill- Treasury Department - Taxation
A. R. Mangus - Federal Emergency Relief Administration, Works Pro-
                 gress Administration - Rural Sociology

John W. Manning - Tennessee Valley Authority - Public Administration
Charles F. Marsh - National Recovery Administration, Employment
           Service - Economics
Mark S. Massel - National Recovery Administration, Works Progress
           Administration - Economics
Stacy May - National Recovery Administration, Department of Labor
           Economics
Robert D. Meade - Department of Interior - American History
Scudder Mekeel - Soil Conservation Service, Department of Interior -
           Social Anthropology
Harold D. Meyer - Works Progress Administration - Sociology
Albert L. Meyers - Department of Agriculture - Economics
Helen Hill Miller - Department of Agriculture - Political Science
Day Monroe - Department of Agriculture - Economics
Carl Henry Monsees - National Recovery Administration - Farm Security
           Administration - Public Administration
R. H. Montgomery - National Resources Commission, Department of
           Agriculture - Political Economy
Loyle A. Morrison - Tariff Commission, National Recovery Administra-
           tion - Economics
William E. Mosher - Federal Power Commission - Public Administration
Howard B. Myers - Works Progress Administration - Labor Economics
Robert J. Myers - Works Progress Administration, Children's Bureau
           - Labor Economics
Richard W. Nelson - Department of Agriculture - Forest Economics
Oswald Nielsen - Departments of Agriculture and Commerce - Economics
Arthur E. Nilsson - Securities and Exchange Commission - Economics
Edgar Burkhardt Nixon - State Department - History
Mildred Northrop - Treasury Department - Economics
William L. Nunn - Civilian Works Administration, Works Progress
           Administration - Economics
Paul H. Nystrom - National Recovery Administration - Economics
Al F. O'Donnell - National Recovery Administration, Treasury
           Department - Economics
William F. Ogburn - National Recovery Administration, National
           Resources Planning Board - Sociology
Gladys L. Palmer - Works Progress Administration, Social Security
           Board - Industrial Relations
Maurice Parmelee - Departments of Agriculture, Interior, and
           Treasury - Economics, Sociology
Rexford C. Parmelee - Department of Commerce, Securities and Exchange
           Commission - Economics
Gutav Peck - National Administration, Department of Labor - Labor
           Economics
J. Roland Pennock - Social Security Board - Political Science
Jacob Perlman - Department of Labor - Economics
Charles Edward Person - National Recovery Administration - Economics
Harlow S. Person - Rural Electrification Association, National
           Resources Committee - Economics

Vernon L. Phelps - Department of State and Agriculture - Economics
W. C. Plummer - Works Progress Administration - Economics
F. W. Powell - National Planning Board - Political Science
Maurice T. Price - Soil Conservation Service - Sociology, Education
C. Herman Pritchett - Tennessee Valley Authority, Department of
            Labor - Public Administration
M. J. Proudfoot - Census Bureau - Statistical Cartography
Robert E. Rapp - Federal Emergency Relief Administration - Economics
B. U. Ratchford - Department of Agriculture - Economics
Carl Raushenbush - National Recovery Administration - Economics
Paul J. Raver - Department of Interior, Tennessee Valley Authority -
            Economics
Vergil D. Reed - Census Bureau - Marketing
George T. Renner - National Resources Planning Board - Geography
Lloyd Rice - State Department, Tariff Commission - Economics
Stuart A. Rice - Census Bureau - Sociology, Statistics
Winfield W. Riefler - Central Statistical Board, National Emergency
            Council - Economics
John R. Riggleman - National Recovery Administration, Bureau of
            Public Roads, Bureau of Agricultural Economics -
            Economics, Statistics
Harold B. Rowe - Department of Agriculture - Economics
William H. Rowe - Department of Agriculture - Agricultural
            Economics
Richard Joel Russell - Soil Conservation Service - Geography
Franklin W. Ryan - Federal Housing Administration - Social Science
Oscar Baxter Ryder - National Recovery Administration - Economics
T. R. Schellenberg - National Archives, Works Progress Administra-
            tion - Modern European History
Carl T. Schmidt - Department of Agriculture - Economics
Charles Seeger - Department of Agriculture, Works Progress
            Administration -Musicology
Gustav Seidler - National Recovery Administration, Department of
            Justice - Economics
B. M. Selekman - Federal Emergency Relief Administration - Industrial
            Relations
Lawrence Howard Seltzer - Departments of Agriculture and Treasury -
            Economics
Vernon G. Setser - National Park Service, National Archives - American
            History
I. L. Sharfman - National Railroad Adjustment Board - Economics
Walter A. Shewhart - Departments of Agriculture and War - Statistics
Henry S. Shryock - Federal Emergency Relief Administration, Census
            Bureau - Demography
Mapheus Smith - Works Progress Administration, Federal Emergency
            Relief Administration - Sociology, Psychology
Mark A. Smith - Tariff Commission - Economics
Milton V. Smith - Tennessee Valley Authority - Public Administration
Raymond C. Smith - Department of Agriculture - Rural Welfare
Constant Southworth - National Recovery Administration State
            Department - Economics

Dade Sparks - Department of Agriculture - History
Estal E. Sparlin - Department of Agriculture - Economics
T. G. Standing - Federal Emergency Relief Administration, Works
          Progress Administration - Sociology
W. H. Stead - Employment Service - Business Economics
M. L. Stecker - Federal Emergency Relief Administration, Works
          Progress Administration, Social Security Board -
          Economics
Frederick F. Stephan - Federal Emergency Relief Administration -
          Statistics, Sociology
Ward Stewart - Tennessee Valley Authority - Political Science
Walter W. Stewart - Treasury Department - Economics
W. Blair Stewart - National Emergency Council, National Resources
          Committee - Economics
Ralph H. Stimson - Departments of Interior and State - Political
          Science
Leroy D. Stinebower - Department of State - International Economic
          Relations
George W. Stocking - National Recovery Administration - Economics
Edward Stone - Department of Agriculture - Money and Banking
N. I. Stone - National Recovery Administration - Economics
R. W. Stone - National Labor Relations Board, National Recovery
          Administration - Labor Economics
Wesley A. Sturges - Department of Agriculture - Law Administration
Stephen Sweeney - Works Progress Administration - Insurance
Carl B. Swisher - Departments of Agriculture and Justice - Political
          Science
Conrad Taeuber - Federal Emergency Relief Administration, Works
          Progress Administration, Department of Agriculture
          - Population
Carl F. Taeusch - Department of Agriculture - Philosophy, Economics
Carl C. Taylor - Departments of Interior and Agriculture - Rural
          Sociology
Paul S. Taylor - Department of Agriculture, Social Security Board -
          Economics
George Terborgh - Federal Reserve Board - Economics
E. D. Tetreau - Federal Emergency Relief Administration - Rural
          Sociology
Dorothy Swaine Thomas - Federal Emergency Relief Administration,
          National Resources Commission - Sociology
Woodlief Thomas - Federal Reserve Board - Economics
Warren S. Thompson - National Resources Board - Population
C. W. Thornthwaite - Soil Conservation Service - Geography
Willard Thorp - National Recovery Administration, Department of
          Commerce - Economics
Clark Tibbitts - Federal Emergency Relief Administration, Public
          Health Service - Public Welfare
L. Deming Tilton - National Resources Planning Board - Planning

Vladimir P. Timoshenko - Department of Agriculture - Economics
James M. Tinley - Department of Agriculture - Agricultural Economics
Ralph B. Tower - Department of Agriculture - Public Finance
Ruth M. Underhill - Department of Agriculture, Indian Affairs -
                Anthropology
Arthur R. Upgren - Census Bureau, Federal Emergency Relief Adminis-
                tration, Works Progress Administration - Economics
Stephen S. Visher - Departments of State and Agriculture - Social
                Geography
Paul L. Vogt - Department of Agriculture - Sociology
Paul W. Wager - Department of Agriculture - Political Science
Warren C. Waite - Department of Agriculture - Agricultural Economics
Herman Walker - Department of Agriculture - Rural Governments
William H. Wandel - National Recovery Administration, Social Security
                Board - Economics
Caroline F. Ware - National Recovery Administration - American History
Frank A. Waring - Tariff Commission - Economics
Earl E. Warner - Department of Agriculture - Political Science
Alfred N. Watson - Census Bureau, Department of Agriculture, Bureau
                of Labor Statistics - Statistics
W. S. Webb - Tennessee Valley Authority - Archeology, Physics
George M. Weber - Bureau of Labor Statistics, Indian Affairs -
                Economics, Statistics
Julius T. Wendzel - Department of Agriculture, Social Security
                Board - Economics
Charles P. White - Tennessee Valley Authority - Finance, Taxation
Max R. White - Department of Agriculture - Public Administration
Wilford L. White - Department of Commerce, Federal Trade Commission -
                Economics
Dean R. Wickes - Soil Conservation Service - Geography
Jeanne Elizabeth Wier - Works Progress Administration - History
Walter W. Wilcox - Department of Agriculture - Agricultural Economics
Kenneth B. Williams - Works Progress Administration - Economics
Lucius Wilmerding, Jr. - Treasury Department - Political Science
Charles M. Wiltse - National Resources Planning Board, National
                Youth Administration - Political Theory
R. S. Winslow - Public Works Administration - Economics
Edwin E. Witte - Commission on Economic Security - Economics,
                Political Science
John B. Wolf - National Park Service - Modern European History
Robert M. Woodbury - National Recovery Administration - Labor
                Statistics
T. J. Woofter - Works Progress Administration - Sociology, Economics
Theodore O. Yntema - National Recovery Administration - Economics
                Statistics
George F. Zook - Bureau of Education - History

REFERENCES

1. Aaron, Daniel. Men of Good Hope. New York: Oxford University
   Press, 1951.

2. "Abbe, Cleveland, Jr." The National Cyclopaedia of American
   Biography. 1937. Vol. XXVI

3. Alsop, Joseph, and Kintner, Robert. Men Around the President.
   New York: Doubleday, Doran and Company, Inc., 1939.

4. Atwood, Albert W. "Government by Professors." Saturday Evening
   Post, October 14, 1933, pp. 23, 87-90.

5. Baker, Gladys L.; Rasmussen, Wayne D.; Wiser, Vivian; and Porter,
   Jane M. Century of Service. Washington, D.C.: United States
   Department of Agriculture, 1963.

6. Barry, David S. Forty Years in Washington. Boston: Little, Brown,
   and Company, 1924.

7. Barzun, Jacques. The American University. New York: Harper and
   Row, 1968.

8. Beard, Charles. The American Leviathan. New York: The Macmillan
   Company, 1931.

9. _____, _____, and Beard, Mary R. The Rise of American Civilization
   Vol. II. New York: The Macmillan Company, 1930.

10. Becker, Carl L. Cornell University: Founders and the Founding.
    Ithaca: Cornell University Press, 1943.

11. Bellush, Bernard. Franklin D. Roosevelt as Governor of New York.
    New York: Columbia University Press. 1955.

12. Benedict, Murray R. Farm Policies of the United States, 1790-
    1953. New York: The Twentieth Century Fund, 1953.

13. Berle, A. A., Jr. "Case for the Professor in Washington." New York
    Times Magazine, February 5, 1961, pp. 17, 84-86.

14. Blaisdell, T. C. The Federal Trade Commission. New York: AMS Press,
    Inc., 1967.

184

185

15. Blythe, Samuel. "Kaleidoscope." Saturday Evening Post, September, 1933, pp. 5-7, 54-55.

16. Bowman, Claude Charleton. The College Professor in America. Philadelphia, Arno Press, 1938.

17. "A Brain Trust at Work." Review of Reviews, July, 1933, pp.20-24.

18. "Brains in Government." Saturday Evening Post, July 28, 1934. p.22.

19. "Brown, Elmer Ellsworth." The National Cyclopaedia of American Biography. 1940. Vol. XXVIII.

20. Brubacher, John S., and Rudy, Willis. Higher Education in Transition. New York: Harper and Row, Publishers, 1968.

21. Bryce, James. The American Commonwealth. Vol. II. New York: Macmillan and Company, 1894.

22. Buck, Paul H., ed., Social Sciences at Harvard. Cambridge: Harvard University Press, 1965.

23. "Burgess, George K." The National Cyclopaedia of American Biography. 1935. Vol. XXIV

24. Burgess, John W. Reminiscences of an American Scholar. New York: Columbia University Press, 1934.

25. Butler, Nicholas Murray. Across the Busy Years. Vol. I. New York: Charles Scribner's Sons, 1939.

26. _____, _____. Across the Busy Years. Vol. II. New York: Charles Scribner's Sons, 1940.

27. Butts, R. Freeman. The College Charts Its Course. New York: McGraw-Hill Book Company, Inc., 1939.

28. Cartensen, Vernon. "The Origin and Early Development of the Wisconsin Idea." Wisconsin Magazine of History, XXXIX (Spring), 1956, 181-87.

29. Cattell, Jaques., ed. Directory of American Scholars, Lancaster: The Science Press, 1942.

30. Childs, Marquis, and Reston, James, ed. Walter Lippmann and His Times. New York: Harcourt, Brace and Company, 1959.

31. Christensen, A. N., and Kirkpatrick, E. M. Running the Country. New York: Henry Holt and Company, 1946.

32. Clarke, F. W. "The Evolution of the American University." Forum, September, 1901, pp. 94-104.

33. "Claxton, Philander Priestly." The National Cyclopaedia of American Biography. 1916. Vol. XV.

34. Coffman, Lotus D. The State University Its Work and Problems. Minneapolis: The University of Minnesota Press, 1934.

35. "College Professors and the Public." Atlantic Monthly, February, 1902, pp. 282-288.

36. "Columbia University Scholars in the Public Service." School and Society, XXXVIII (November 11, 1933), 642-644.

37. "The Common Welfare." The Survey, January 7, 1911, pp. 517-520.

38. Commons, John R. Myself. New York: The Macmillan Company, 1934.

39. Conant, James B. "America Remakes the University." Atlantic Monthly, May, 1964, pp. 41-45.

40. "Cooper, William John." The National Cyclopaedia of American Biography. 1940. Vol. XXVIII.

41. Cowley, W. H. "European Influences Upon American Higher Education." Educational Record, XX (April, 1939), 165-190.

42. Crane, R. T. The Utility of all Kinds of Higher Schooling. Chicago, 1909.

43. Cremin, Lawrence A. The Transformation of the School. New York: Random House, 1961.

44. Cunliffe, Marcus. "The Intellectuals: The United States." Encounter, May, 1955, pp. 23-33.

45. Curti, Merle. American Paradox. Brunswick: Rutgers University Press, 1956.

46. _____, _____, ed., American Scholarship. New York: Russell and Russell, 1967.

47. _____, _____. The Growth of American Thought. New York: Harper and Brothers, 1943.

48. _____, _____. "Intellectuals and Other People." American Historical Review, LX (January, 1955), 259-280.

49. Cushman, Robert E. The Independent Regulatory Commissions: New York; Oxford University Press, 1941.

50. Dallek, Robert. Democrat and Diplomat. New York: Oxford University Press, 1968.

51. Dana, Samuel Trask. Forest and Range Policy. New York: McGraw-Hill Book Company, Inc., 1956.

52. Daniels, Josephus. The Wilson Era: Years of War and After, 1917-1923. Chapel Hill: The University of North Carolina Press, 1946.

53. Davis, Chester C. "Place of Farmers, Economists and Administrators in Developing Agricultural Policy." Journal of Farm Economics, XXII (February, 1940), 1-7.

54. Davis, Forrest. "The Rise of the Commissars." New Outlook, December, 1933, pp. 23-26.

55. "The Demobilized Professor." Atlantic Monthly, April, 1919, pp. 537-545.

56. "Dixon, Roland B." The National Cyclopaedia of American Biography. 1954. Vol. XXXIX.

57. Draper, Andrew S. "American Universities and the National Life." National Education Association Proceedings, (Vol. 37). (1898), 103-122.

58. "Durand, Edward Dana." The National Cyclopaedia of American Biography. 1910. Vol. XIV.

59. "The Editor's Easy Chair." Harper's Magazine, March 8, 1958, pp. 18-19.

60. Eliot, Charles W. "The New Education." Atlantic Monthly, February, 1869, pp. 203-220.

61. Elliott, William Yandell. The Need for Constitutional Reform. New York: McGraw-Hill Book Company, Inc., 1935.

62. Ely, Richard T. Ground Under Our Feet. New York: Macmillan Company, 1938.

63. "Emery, Hency C." The National Cyclopaedia of American Biography. 1931. Vol. XXI.

64. "Everett, Edward." Dictionary of American Biography, 1931, Vol.VI.

65. Farley, James A. Jim Farley's Story. New York: McGraw-Hill Book Company, Inc., 1948.

66. "Felix Frankfurter." Fortune, January, 1936, pp. 63, 87-90.

67. "Fess, Simeon D." The National Cyclopaedia of American Biography. 1939. Vol, XXVII.

68. Fine, Sidney. Laissez-Faire and the General-Welfare State. Ann Arbor: University of Michigan Press, 1956.

69. Fischer, Louis. "Social Change in the Brain Trust." Nation, May 31, 1933, pp. 604-5.

70. Flexner, Abraham. The American College. New York: The Century Company, 1908.

71. Forrestal, James. "The University in Public Service." Journal of Higher Education, XVII (January, 1947), 1-6.

72. Franklin, Jay. Remaking America. Boston: Houghton Mifflin Company, 1942.

73. Freidin, Seymour and Bailey, George. The Experts. New York: Macmillan Company, 1968.

74. Fuess, Claude M. Calvin Coolidge: The Man from Vermont. Hamden, Connecticut: Archon Books, 1965.

75. Fusfeld, Daniel R. The Economic Thought of Franklin D. Roosevelt and the Origins of the New Deal. New York: Columbia University Press, 1956.

76. Gabriel, Ralph Henry. American Democratic Thought. New York: The Ronald Press Company, 1940.

77. Garraty, John A. Henry Cabot Lodge. New York: Alfred A. Knopf, 1953.

78. Gerould, Gordon Hall. "The Professor and the Wide, Wide World." Scribner's, April, 1919, pp. 465-470.

79. Goldman, Eric F. Rendezvous With Destiny. New York: Alfred A. Knopf, 1952.

80. Graham, Otis L., Jr. An Encore for Reform. New York: Oxford University Press, 1967.

81. Grattan, C. Hartley. "The Historians Cut Loose." American Mercury, August, 1927, pp. 414-430.

82. Griswold, Alfred Whitney. In the University Tradition. New Haven: Yale University Press, 1957.

83. Gurko, Leo. Heroes, Highbrows and the Popular Mind. Indianapolis: The Bobbs-Merrill Company, Inc., 1953.

84. Hadley, Arthur Twining. "What is Education?" Harper's, December, 1922, pp. 14-22.

85. Hard, William. "Sidelights on the New Cabinet." Review of Reviews, April, 1929, pp. 53-58.

86. Harding, T. Swann. Two Blades of Grass. Norman: University of Oklahoma Press, 1947.

87. Harris, William Torrey. "The Use of Higher Education." Educational Review, XVI (September, 1898), 147-161.

88. "Harris, William Torrey." Dictionary of American Biography. 1932. Vol. IV.

89. Herbst, Jurgen. The German Historical School in American Scholarship. Ithaca: Cornell University Press, 1965.

90. Herring, E. Pendleton. Federal Commissioners. Cambridge: Harvard University Press, 1936.

91. Hicks, John D. Republican Ascendancy. New York: Harper and Brothers, 1960.

92. "Hill, David Jayne." The National Cyclopaedia of American Biography. 1904. Vol. XII.

93. Hinshaw, David. Herbert Hoover: American Quaker. New York: Farrar, Straus and Company, 1950.

94. Hofstadter, Richard. Anti-intellectualism in American Life. New York: Alfred A. Knopf, 1963.

95. _____, _____, and Hardy, C. DeWitt. The Development and Scope of Higher Education in the United States. New York: Columbia University Press, 1952.

96. _____, _____, and Metzger, Walter P. The Development of Academic Freedom in the United States. New York: Columbia University Press, 1952.

97. Hoover, Calvin. Memoirs of Capitalism, Communism, and Nazism. Durham: Duke University Press, 1965.

98. Hoover, Herbert. Memoirs: The Cabinet and the Presidency 1920-1933. New York: Macmillan Company, 1952.

99. House, Edward Mandell, and Seymour, Charles. What Really Happened at Paris. New York: Charles Scribner's Sons, 1921.

100. Houston, David F. Eight Years With Wilson's Cabinet 1913 to 1920. Vol. I. Garden City: Doubleday, Page and Company, 1926.

101. _____, _____. Eight Years With Wilson's Cabinet 1913 to 1920. New York: Doubleday, Page and Company, 1926. Vol. II.

102. Howe, Frederic C. Wisconsin An Experiment in Democracy. New York: Charles Scribner's Sons, 1912.

103. "Hoxie, Robert F." The National Cyclopaedia of American Biography. 1933. Vol. XXIII.

104. Hugh-Jones, E. M. Woodrow Wilson and American Liberalism. New York: Macmillan Company, 1948.

105. "Immigration." The Survey, January 7, 1911, pp. 571-602.

106. James, Edmund J. "The Function of the State University." Science, November 17, 1905, pp. 609-628.

107. "Jeremiah W. Jenks." American Economic Review, XIX (December, 1929), 745.

108. Jesse, Richard Henry. "The Function of the State University." National Education Association Proceedings, (Vol. 40). (1901), 606-613.

109. Jordan, David Starr. The Trend of the American University. Stanford: Stanford University Press, 1929.

110. Kelly, Robert L. "The American College and the Great War." Scribner's, January, 1918, pp. 77-83.

111. King, Clyde Lyndon. "The Public Services of the College and University Expert." Annals of the American Academy of Political and Social Science, LXVII (September, 1916), 291-296.

112. Kirkendall, Richard S. "A Professor in Farm Politics." Mid-America, XLI (October, 1959), 210-217.

113. Kirkendall, Richard S. "Franklin D. Roosevelt and the Service Intellectual." Mississippi Valley Historical Review, LXIX (December, 1962), 456-471.

114. "Klein, Julius H." The National Cyclopaedia of American Biography. 1930. Vol. C.

115. Krock, Arthur. Memoirs: Sixty Years on the Firing Line. New York: Funk and Wagnalls, 1968.

116. Lasch, Christopher. The New Radicalism in America 1889-1963. New York: Alfred A. Knopf, 1965.

117. Laughlin, J. Laurence. The Federal Reserve Act: Its Origin and Problems. New York: Macmillan Company, 1933.

118. Lemons, J. Stanley. "The Sheppard-Towner Act: Progressivism in the 1920's." Journal of American History, LX (March, 1969), 771-786.

119. Leuchtenburg, William E. "Anti-Intellectualism: An Historical Perspective." Journal of Social Issues, XI (September, 1955), 8-17.

120. Lindley, Ernest K. The Roosevelt Revolution. New York: The Viking Press, 1933.

121. _____, _____. "War on the Brains Trust." Scribner's Magazine, November, 1933, pp. 257-266.

122. Link, Arthur S. Wilson: The Road to the White House. Princeton: Princeton University Press, 1947.

123. _____, _____. Woodrow Wilson and the Progressive Era, 1910-1917. New York: Harper and Brothers, 1954.

124. _____, _____, Wilson: The New Freedom. Princeton: Princeton University Press, 1956.

125. _____, _____, American Epoch. New York: Alfred A. Knopf, 1958.

126. Lippmann, Walter. "The Scholar in a Troubled World." Atlantic Monthly, August, 1932, pp. 148-152.

127. _____, _____. Public Opinion. New York: The Macmillan Company, 1945.

128. Lipset, Seymour Martin. Political Man. New York: Doubleday and Company, Inc., 1960.

129. Literary Digest. "The Hullabaloo Over the Brain Trust."
        June 3, 1933, pp. 8-9.

130. Lovett, Robert Morss. All Our Years. New York: The Viking
        Press, 1948.

131. McCarthy, Charles. The Wisconsin Idea. New York: The Macmillan
        Company, 1912.

132. McCoy, Donald R. Calvin Coolidge The Quiet President. New York
        Macmillan Company, 1967.

133. MacDonald, William. The Intellectual Worker and His Work.
        New York: The Macmillan Company, 1924.

134. McKee, Oliver, Jr. "Professors Put to the Test." North
        American Review, October, 1934, pp. 340-345.

135. Matthews, Brander. "Literary Men and Public Affairs." North
        American Review, April, 1909, pp. 527-538.

136. "Mead, Elwood." The National Cyclopaedia of American Biography.
        1930. Vol. A.

137. "Merriam, C. Hart." The National Cyclopaedia of American
        Biography. 1906. Vol. XIII.

138. Merritt, Albert N. War Time Control of Distribution of Foods.
        New York: Macmillan Company, 1920.

139. Mitchell, Jonathan. "Don't Shoot the Professors!" Harpers
        Magazine, May, 1934, pp. 740-49.

140. Moley, Raymond. After Seven Years. New York: Harper and
        Brothers Publishers, 1939.

141. "Moore, John Bassett." The National Cyclopaedia of American
        Biography. 1909. Vol. XI.

142. Morrill, James Lewis. The Ongoing State University. Minneapolis:
        The University of Minnesota Press, 1960.

143. Mowry, George E. The Era of Theodore Roosevelt. New York:
        Harper and Brothers, 1958.

144. Mullendore, William Clinton. History of the United States Food
        Administration, 1917-1919. Stanford: Stanford University
        Press, 1941.

145. Myers, William S. and Newton, Walter H. The Hoover Administration, A Documented Narrative. New York: Charles Scribner's Sons, 1936.

146. Nevins, Allan. The State Universities and Democracy. Urbana: University of Illinois Press, 1962.

147. Norton, Hugh S. "Economists in Government, Changing Patterns." Business Economics, IV (September, 1969), 85-88.

148. Nye, Russel B. Midwestern Progressive Politics. East Lansing: Michigan State College Press, 1951.

149. Pringle, Henry F. Theodore Roosevelt. New York: Harcourt, Brace and Company, 1931.

150. _____, _____. The Life and Times of William Howard Taft. New York: Farrar and Rhinehart, Inc., 1939. Vol. I.

151. _____, _____. The Life and Times of William Howard Taft. New York: Farrar and Rhinehart, Inc., 1939. Vol. II.

152. Pritchett, H. S. "The Relation of Educated Men to the State." Science, November, 1900, pp. 657-666.

153. "Professors and Politics." School and Society. XXXVI (October 1, 1932), 429-430.

154. "Professors at Washington." Christian Century, May 31, 1933, pp. 711-12.

155. "President Roosevelt's Academic Advisors." School and Society XXXVII (April 15, 1933), 497.

156. Rader, Benjamin G. The Academic Mind and Reform. Lexington: University of Kentucky Press, 1966.

157. "Ripley, William Z." The National Cyclopaedia of American Biography. 1945. Vol. XXXII.

158. "Roberts, Owen Josephus." The National Cyclopaedia of American Biography. 1930. Vol. A

159. "Rogers, James Harvey." The National Cyclopaedia of American Biography. 1944. Vol. XXI.

160. Rogers, Lindsey. "The Professor and Public Service." Educational Record, XIX (January, 1938), 12-22.

161. Rogers, Walter P. Andrew D. White and the Modern University.
     Ithaca: Cornell University Press, 1942.

162. Roosevelt, Theodore. An Autobiography. New York: Macmillan
     Company, 1919.

163. _____, _____. "On the Rewards of Scholarship." Science,
     July 7, 1905, pp. 27-28.

164. Rosenman, Samuel I. Working With Roosevelt. New York: Harper
     and Brothers, 1952.

165. Roper, Daniel C. Fifty Years of Public Life. Durham: Duke
     University Press, 1941.

166. Rudolph, Frederick. The American College and University. New
     York: Alfred A. Knopf, 1962.

167. Salomon, Leon I., ed. The Independent Federal Regulatory
     Agencies. New York: The H. W. Wilson Company, 1959.

168. Schlesinger, Arthur M., Jr. The Age of Roosevelt: The Crisis
     of the Old Order. Boston: Houghton Mifflin Company, 1957.

169. _____, _____. The Age of Roosevelt: The Coming of the
     New Deal. Boston: Houghton Mifflin Company, 1959.

170. _____, _____. The Age of Roosevelt: The Politics of
     Upheaval. Boston: Houghton Mifflin Company, 1960.

171. Shaw, Roger. "Brain Trusts of History." Review of Reviews,
     June, 1934, pp. 25-26, 54.

172. Shotwell, James T. At the Paris Peace Conference. New York:
     Macmillan Company, 1937.

173. "Silcox, Ferdinand Augustus." The National Cyclopaedia of
     American Biography. 1941. Vol. XXIX.

174. Slosson, Edwin E. Great American Universities. New York:
     The Macmillan Company, 1910.

175. "Smith, George Otis." The National Cyclopaedia of American
     Biography. 1949. Vol. XXXV.

176. "Some Diplomats and a Senator." The Outlook, April 29, 1911,
     pp. 946-947.

177. Stearns, Harold. Liberalism in America. New York: Boni
     and Liveright, Inc., 1919.

178. Steffens, Lincoln. "Sending a State to College." The American Magazine, February, 1909, pp. 349-364.

179. Sternsher, Bernard. Rexford Tugwell and the New Deal. New Brunswick: Rutgers University Press, 1964.

180. "Stockberger, Warner W." The National Cyclopaedia of American Biography. 1949. Vol. XXXV.

181. "Stratton, Samuel W." The National Cyclopaedia of American Biography. 1906. Vol. XIII.

182. Stuart, Graham H. The Department of State: A History of Its Organization Procedure, and Personnel. New York: The Macmillan Company, 1949.

183. Taylor, Henry C. "Early History of Agricultural Economics." Journal of Farm Economics, XXII (February, 1940), 84-97.

184. Terrell, John Upton. The United States Department of Agriculture. New York: Duell, Sloan and Pearce, 1966.

185. Thwing, Charles Franklin. The American and the German University. New York: The Macmillan Company, 1928.

186. "Tigert, John James." The National Cyclopaedia of American Biography. 1934. Vol. D.

187. Tugwell, Rexford G. The Democratic Roosevelt. Garden City: Doubleday and Company, Inc., 1957.

188. Turner, Frederick Jackson. The Frontier in American History. New York: Henry Holt and Company, 1947.

189. "VanDevanter, Willis." The National Cyclopaedia of American Biography. 1934. Vol. D.

190. Van Hise, Charles R. "The Place of the University in a Democracy." National Education Association Proceedings, LIV (1916),68-73.

191. _____, _____. "The War Work of the University of Wisconsin." Review of Reviews, July, 1918, pp. 67-69.

192. Van Metre, Thurman W. Economic History of the United States. New York: Henry Holt and Company, 1921.

193. Veysey, Laurence R. "The Academic Mind of Woodrow Wilson." Mississippi Valley Historical Review, LXIX (March, 1963), 613-634.

194. Veysey, Laurence R. The Emergence of the American University. Chicago: The University of Chicago Press, 1965.

195. Villard, O. G. "The Idealist Comes to the Front." Nation. October 4, 1933. p. 371.

196. "Walker, Francis." The National Cyclopaedia of American Biography. 1955. Vol. XL.

197. Walworth, Arthur. Woodrow Wilson: American Prophet. New York: Longmans, Green and Company, 1958.

198. _____, _____. Woodrow Wilson: World Prophet. New York: Longmans, Green and Company, 1958.

199. Warne, Frank Julian. The Tide of Immigration. New York: D. Appleton and Company, 1916.

200. Wesley, Edgar Bruce. Proposed: The University of the United States. Minneapolis: University of Minnesota Press, 1936.

201. "White, Andrew D." The National Cyclopaedia of American Biography. 1897. Vol. IV.

202. White, Leonard D. Trends in Public Administration. New York: McGraw-Hill Book Company, Inc., 1933.

203. _____, _____. ed., The Future of Government in the United States. Chicago: The University of Chicago Press, 1942.

204. "Who Willed American Participation." New Republic, April 14, 1917, pp. 308-310.

205. Wilbur, Ray Layman, and Hyde, Arthur Mastick. The Hoover Policies. New York: Charles Scribner's Sons, 1937.

206. Wiley, Harvey W. An Autobiography. Indianapolis: The Bobbs-Merrill Company, 1930.

207. "Willis, Frank Bartlett." The National Cyclopaedia of American Biography. 1931, Vol. XXI.

208. "Willis, H. Parker." The National Cyclopaedia of American Biography. 1940. Vol. XXVIII.

209. "Willoughby, W. F." The National Cyclopaedia of American Biography. 1930. Vol. A.

210. Wilson, Logan. The Academic Man. New York: Oxford University Press, 1942.

INDEX